Digital
Monsters

Dr Vivian Asimos

Clink
Street

London | New York

Published by Clink Street Publishing 2020

Copyright © 2020

First edition.

ISBNs:
978-1-913568-19-1 Paperback
978-1-913568-20-7 Ebook

Chapter 1

Introducing the Monsters
of the Digital Worlds

My face is only lit by the soft blue glow of the screen, continued through the constantly renewed promise that, after this story, I will sleep. But with each story, the dark encroaches closer and closer, until it feels the closeness of a screen is the only comfort. The radiators click with the soft noise of the slow cooling of the boiler resting for the night. Each noise makes my eyes dart around the ever-darkening room in sudden fear the horror from the screen is suddenly there, lurking somewhere in the darkened corners of the room.

But the fear continues to creep even after the new dawn. Walking home at twilight, the trees linger a little closer, replaying the narratives which suddenly feel more telling and closer to home. I glance twice at moving shadows.

And I start to believe that monsters are real.

Monsters have captured the human imagination since human imagination came into being. From vampires to werewolves, every culture carries its own monsters, bringing them into different times and locations with the movement of peoples and societies. Monsters are an intricate part of the human experience. Monsters haunt us because they are us. It is easy for us to see monsters as unimportant simply because they are not real. But monsters *are* real.

Now, I do not mean monsters are real in the sense that,

when I am walking along the forest path, I truly expect some Lovecraftian nightmare to suddenly jump out at me from the seemingly encroaching dark forests. But there is a reason why they scare me – there's a reason the monster still haunts me, even though I may think of them as not physically around me. Let's start, for example, with a simple case of zombies. Zombies, despite their current position in popular culture as slowly shambling reanimated dead, have their origins in Haitian Vodou, a religious practice that is an amalgamation of Christianity and traditional African beliefs. The Zombies in Haitian Vodou are people animated and enslaved to serve for another as a labourer. At the heart of the fear of zombies is a fear of re-enslavement by a people who had suffered tremendously under the yoke of slavery. In the shadow of slavery, the zombie is real. It carries with it the real memory of a cultural scar.

Monsters carry in them cultural memories and social anxieties. And digital monsters are no different. If I asked anyone who participates in the creation and retelling of horror narratives online if they believed in the existence of their monsters, I would be laughed out of whatever virtual room I had been in. However, we can phrase the question differently: does your monster have an effect on the way you understand yourself and your world?

This question is at the heart of everything. Because monsters can be real in a different sense to a physical real presence to their form. The oft conceived binary difference between reality and fiction is problematic, and has the resulting idea that something fictional is not worth detailed discussion, especially academically. But this is a false dichotomy – something can be both fictional and real simultaneously. Monsters are often in a middle ground between the two worlds, and are especially troubling the dichotomy in the digital world. But most importantly, monsters are real through the effect they have on the cultures and societies which tell them. Monsters are real in their impact on the storytellers and story-cultures.

Like their dislike of the dichotomy of reality and fiction, monsters demonstrate the limits and boundaries of the societies and cultures which they belong to. And most importantly, the monsters are the direct result of our categorical systems failing. We, as humans, enjoy categorising the world around us. We see things as belonging to certain systems. As we grow, we learn the word dog. And animals that look different all belong to the word "dog". Similarly, we point at other people and see them as belonging to word "like me" or "like them". We point at things that are alive and call them "alive", and these things are set apart from the things we point at and see as "dead". We have these mental boxes we sort things into, all labelled and filed away in neat boxes. Every culture and society has a way of ordering their life and understanding. Monsters demonstrate their disruption.

We can sometimes see this in their physical form. Take, for instance, the griffin. The griffin has the back half of a lion, and the front half of an eagle. The form of the griffin is neither bird nor big cat, breaking our categories of what animal it really is. It also breaks our geological categories. It is of both land and air, breaking our understanding of where certain animals reside and understandings of what these geological locations mean. Similarly, the centaur breaks the categorical distinctions between human and animal. The monstrous form demonstrates a break with what we are accustomed to and destroys our categorical considerations.

Monsters can also break categories in the way they interact with the world and others in it. The vampire, for instance, is not monstrous in its physical form, but it is monstrous in how it exists and interacts with the world. It breaks down the categorical distinction between life and death – two social categories which should never cross. Not only are they the living dead, but they take the living and strip them of life force – blood – bringing them closer to the side of death. They begin the breaking of boundaries and categorical distinctions in their existence and their actions. Werewolves are not only breaking the physical form boundaries by shifting between animal and human – two categories typically left uncrossed – but also in their actions. They force the transgression onto others through their bite.

Jeffrey Cohen, an essential founder of what became Monster Studies, wrote of the monster as a harbinger of categorical crisis. Monsters demonstrate these categorical breakdowns, and they demonstrate to us the inherent fear we have in our cultural categories breaking. If there is a creature that breaks our understanding of the strict separation between the worlds of life and death, what does that mean for our understanding of our own lives? How we associate with those who have passed before us? Our understanding of religion and family, and many other cultural institutions, will shift. The foundations of which we built our understanding shifts.

Whether or not a vampire physically is present in the world is different than whether or not it's *real*. Monsters are real in the effect they have on us, the categorical breakdowns they represent, and the anxieties and fears they unveil. They demonstrate to us the drawn boundary lines we paint and just how faded that paint can be. The greatest solace monsters like vampires and werewolves can give us is the comfort that they are not physically present. Our categories can maintain their false boundaries if they are not physically real. But their conceptualised form demonstrates just how scared we are that it will all fall apart around us.

The digital monsters are no different. They are the new monsters – the new vampires and new werewolves – that demonstrate the faded boundaries between new categories and new understandings which have arisen over the years of virtual growth. It paints new categorical fears. But the structures and anxieties are also sometimes the same. The digital worlds are not all that different than the non-digital.

The Anthropological Approach

I have spent the last several years of my life studying monsters from the point of view of an anthropologist. As an anthropologist, I see monsters as cultural artefacts, like clay pots and tapestries. And like other cultural artefacts, studying monsters gives us a look into the cultures that create the monsters and tell their stories. Digital monsters are our contemporary myths, folklore and legends, and these stories tell us about how the online world thinks, feels, and acts.

Anthropologists are annoying, and we define our primary method of research by its annoyance. We sit and list endless questions about every aspect of everything – we try to revert back to infancy, to point at anything basic and ask "what" and "why" until who we are speaking to are simply sick of us. And then we ask someone else. And during this whole time, we sit back and we watch. We observe what people are doing, and then we try and do it too. We do what is called "participant observation". Anthropology, at its heart, is a collection of questions about simple things in life: why we wear what we wear when we wear it; what we say when we say it and how we say it. We prod questions immensely with little apparent end in sight – always anchoring everything to something we can see or hear from the community itself. We go into a community like children who are eager to learn everything we can about how life is structured, and why it is structured that way.

Many anthropologists see their field sites as remote locations. They load a backpack up with essentials, a voice recorder, maybe a camera and a journal. They grab a machete and they trek into the wildernesses, eager to live in small villages they hope the world has never heard from before. I, on the other hand, find my field site online. I do not trek with a machete, but with a laptop and a highspeed internet connection. I believe there is a lot to learn from every community, not just the ones who live in remote locations in the world. There is something interesting about people, fundamentally, and this does not change with the use of highspeed internet and online chat rooms. Some unknown community is not the only one who still tells interesting stories – we all do.

This book is a reflection of anthropology when it comes to monsters – what is the monster doing for the community it represents? What effect does the monster impart to those who tell it, share it, and created it? How do the monsters impact the world that tells them?

The Digital World

The online world is full of nomadic groups: shifting from settlement to settlement. Individuals branch off from groups; sometimes they then join others, but other times they draw others to them to come up with their own new nomadic group. From above, it can appear almost as clouds; there are masses individuals can join, dispel from and re-join at their leisure, or as the wind blows them. This is why it can be difficult to discuss the idea of an overarching "digital culture". Understanding the internet as a cohesive group is a gross misunderstanding of what makes the internet interesting and inherently human.

I often find the idea of a "digital culture" being referred to, accepted, but never defended or questioned. The idea of a cohesive culture is a given, and not just in academic literature. The idea of a "gaming culture" is frequently referred to in video game circles, or even "nerd culture" more generally; it is referred to on podcasts, Let's Plays and other web videos, and can be found frequently in discussions on forum sites like reddit. For everyone, the presence of a "digital culture" is taken for granted. Is digital culture separate from nondigital culture, or is gaming culture a subculture? And where does nerd culture fit into this?

I find these questions unnecessarily confusing and, quite frankly, missing the point. I prefer to think of digital communities – a plural to reflect the multiplicity possible. One can trace similarities in community groups close to one another, but it becomes difficult the further away from the initial place of research one gets. However, individuals may move easily, flowing into a new position. Sometimes it takes time to learn the nuances of a new communal group, but sometimes the inherent differences are easy to find quicker. But the ease of movement does not necessarily mean there is one coherent community group with smaller subgroups. Rather, it speaks more to the nature of the environment and an individual's intelligence to pick up on small changes in social norms.

At the heart of these kinds of conversations is the idea that the digital world, and the online environment, is somehow inherently different than anything else in existence. Somehow, people no longer act the way people act where the internet is involved. But this, quite frankly, is unrealistic. Often, we forget that on the other side of the username is a person. The context of the online environment may cause differences in communication and lingo – but this is normal when we move to a new space, even physically.

I will use different language and approaches when talking with my mother than I would when talking with academic colleagues, which are both vastly different than the way I speak to my husband. Similarly, I will speak and approach communication differently when on Facebook than I am on reddit, both of which is vastly different than 4chan. If I spoke to my work colleagues the way I would my husband, I would be considered massively inappropriate.

Trevor Blank, who studied the connections between online storytelling and folklore, said that there may be some differences between the online and offline environments, but that their similarities are also worth noting. Both have customs, set language constructions, neighbourhoods, ways of conveying emotion, commerce, education and even crimes.

My work, and particularly how this book will progress, assumes that people engaging online are people – people who are telling stories. And storytelling is fundamentally human; myths, folklore and legends have circulated among many groups in many areas of the world. Humans are storytelling machines; we are narratives wrapped in flesh. We understand ourselves through narratives, we relate to other people through narratives, we describe ourselves through narratives. Our communities are built on narratives, whether they be physical or digital. We can learn a lot about ourselves and our communities by really looking at our narratives.

Memes are an example of online narratives, and digital mass communal storytelling. Memes, a term originally derived from Richard Dawkins, have come to be defined by their ability to widely spread and the capacity for the individual to express creativity. A meme is not a single video or image, but a multitude, so in order to fully understand a meme, one must see many versions. They are often sparked by one event or post, which then spins into a much larger phenomenon.

Memes can also be inspired by political events, such as the United States presidential nominee Mitt Romney referring to his "binder full of women" in 2012. They can also be spurred on by moments in popular culture, like Kanye West interrupting Taylor Swift at the Video Music Awards in 2009. Kanye Interrupts led to a series of images of Kanye interrupting various moments in history. Let's take Twitch Plays Pokémon as an example of mass meme creation. In 2014, an anonymous programmer hooked up an emulator of the video game *Pokémon Red* to the streaming platform twitch.tv. The emulator was programmed to respond to the chat's input commands, resulting in several thousand players all attempting to play the same game at the same time. The result was utter chaos, with over one million people participating, and over 36 million total views. Factions of the community went to separate forums to plot strategies for greatest success. Some of these utilised elements of the game in order to calm the chaos. These plans often resulted in a certain patter in the chaos which users, inevitably, sketched out as if a mythology. Users wrote and drew memes which praised the benevolent Helix Fossil, which seemed to always be referenced in the chaos.

Online storytelling is massive in its endeavour. It frequently relies on multiple users in many locations to take the initial idea and shift it for themselves, reproducing so then it will be understood, shifted, and reproduced again. Online mass storytelling is cyclical often reproducing itself and its points over and over, told in new and different ways each time. Its reliance on events are as a uniting factor: the community understands the inciting event because it is part of the community's own history. Therefore, shifting it, or remixing it, is adding to the community's own historical narrative. Twitch Plays Pokémon is no longer a one-time event with archived footage on YouTube, it is also comprised of the narratives produced. You cannot understand Twitch Plays Pokémon without also understanding the praise of the Helix Fossil, and the condemning of the false prophet Flareon.

Memes are often considered humorous in nature, as Limor Shifman points out in her book *Memes in Digital Culture*. But memes do not necessarily have to be funny. Horror storytelling online follows a similar format to that already described: reliance on an inciting event, a shifting of the narrative, and an ability for the shifting to be reproduced in new and interesting ways each time an individual imprints themselves to the narrative. Many of the horror stories in this book are told through a massive collective of community members.

The Structure of Online Horror

It's difficult to paint a singular way in which all online horror narratives are structured. Even if we were successful at finding one, things would change and shift, and our understanding suddenly lost to a historical understanding of those pesky old horror narratives which are no longer relevant. This is, at its heart, the most difficult thing about studying the internet: things can change so quickly that your contemporary research can become historical overnight. This being said, I think many of the structures laced into the depictions and writings of online horror are both indicative of the online environment while also echoing structures which have existed in horror literature previously.

To make my primary point about the continuance of structure, I call on a favourite Gothic novel: *Frankenstein*.

Frankenstein was my first personal experience of monster literature in a more classic sense, and I remember being surprised by how familiar it felt to read. It wasn't until far later in life, when I was sketching out my research on online horror, when I saw why it was so familiar. *Frankenstein*, like many other Gothic novels of the time, utilises an epistemological frame: the book is told through a series of diary entries. For its time, this was the way to create a sense of reality to the narrative. This has not changed with contemporary online horror.

Most online narratives attempt to paint a realism to the way narratives are told and read by the audience, using photoshopped images, pseudo-emails and faked government documents to echo an essence of reality to the narratives they tell. Like our older Gothic novel by Mary Shelley, the audience is not fooled to the extent of complete belief in the historical accuracy of the narratives. Rather, the horror is in how real it *feels*. The Gothic novelist works to wrench the reader into a sense of believability never thought possible.

The responses at the time were appalled at such leaps of the audience's belief. Some novels reacted by depicting the heroine as captured within her own delusional imagination, believing each novel she reads as factual. James Beattie, writing in 1783, stated that reading such novels has the consequence of filling "the mind with extravagant thoughts and too often with criminal propensities." Such extreme reactions to popular culture should be of no surprise, as it seems to occur with every new form of art or experience. Rock music was blamed at one point in time, and in more recent years it has become video games and the internet as the loci of youthful corruption.

And here we reach the main point of horror writing, both in *Frankenstein* and in creepypastas online, a theme which will be appearing throughout this book in its explanations and explorations of the world of online horror. We would often explain away these reactions by saying they are appealing to suspension of disbelief. Suspension of disbelief is a wide-spread concept, acknowledging how the audience is willing to go into a movie, book or video game. It's supposed to explain why we gasp when something surprising happens or scream when something horrific happens. It's supposed to explain why, for instance, I start giggling excitedly when I read *The Dresden Files*, and Harry Dresden arrives with a smart quip and a cool trap.

But I think suspension of disbelief misses the point of fiction and the way we interact with it. I do not pick up the next *Dresden* book with an active thought that this is fiction, and I will now push away my overwhelming cynicism in order to enjoy something. Disbelief is not my initial state when I pick up a book, nor my natural inclination. I *want* to believe, however temporarily, that someone as cool and protecting as Harry Dresden exists. When I pick up *Frankenstein*, I want to be shocked and potentially horrified. When I pick up a video game, I am not looking for an out – I am looking for an *in*.

It is not a suspension of disbelief. It is a willingness to believe.

The epistemological framing of *Frankenstein* plays into this – giving me the in at the very beginning. When I go to horror storytelling places online, I am not looking to remove my constant state of disbelief, I go in with an as-if attitude already in place.

This is potentially why horror as a genre is so enticing and strange, while at the same time being of such great discomfort to those who reject it. It's too easy to play as-if the monster is real. As Noël Carroll writes, horror is, by its nature, paradoxical: it can be pleasurable, but only when it causes disquiet and displeasure. It directly plays with our willingness to believe, forcing us to see the world in a way which is surprising and terrible. Joyce Tompkins wrote of those who write supernatural horror in Gothic that these authors enjoy the tactic of forcing the reader from scepticism to belief, through a tug of sudden shocks in how they write the supernatural. However, I don't think these sudden shocks force us from scepticism to belief, but rather they are the process of us realising that we are all in, and how in we are can be horrifying.

The epistemological framing assists in keeping the as-if mind engaged. The role of journals in *Frankenstein* is to lull the reader to remain in their belief by relying on sources used as proof and history. The book reads almost like a catalogue of history, a record of the way things work. Online horror storytelling utilises the structure in the same way as Mary Shelley. The narratives are structured to echo what others use to find proof or historical notes.

Due to the nature of online storytelling, as compared to a set novel, the retaining of belief requires an engagement with the audience mimicking belief. Writers present their work to encourage this form of belief engagement. Users on the Something Awful forum which gave birth to the Slender Man in 2009, for instance, would not just post a photoshopped picture – they would include information on where they "found" such a picture. This is often called an "in-character" form of communication. Like people playing a table-top role-playing game, such as Dungeons and Dragons, users play the role of the character who believes in the sincerity of the narrative. Instead of writing "I like your story, can you write another?", I would instead write, "Oh my god, this is crazy. Give us updates!" In character communication works to continue the role of belief in the user and continue to push the willingness to believe.

More importantly, in-character communication allows

users to *play* with their belief. Because users are beginning their engagement with the narratives already from a standpoint of as-if-real, the continued play within the communication about and for the narrative means users are able to play with their own believability. Their willingness to believe is taken and dwelled in – it thrives on the manipulation inherent in the communication and extends it through the relationship the narrative has with both those who tell it, and those who read it.

Belief, as a word used both colloquially and in academic thought, is considered to be a solid thing. We believe, or we don't believe. It was not until more recently that academics in the study of religion have begun to question the assumptions hidden in the word belief, particularly the apparent solidity to the word. Sociologist Abby Day was especially interested in exploring this, devoting a chapter in her book *Believing in Belonging* to questioning the apparent reliance on the word belief without thought to the assumptions we pile on. Day's own work does not assume belief is a granted when it comes to understanding religion and a person's connection to a religious group.

An important note for our own purposes is the concept of belief as malleable. And not just because it better reflects what happens in the digital world, but because it also better reflects how beliefs work in more traditional places of belief function: religion. During my time studying Christian Science, a religion known for its rejection of mainstream medication, I witnessed a believer taking an ibuprofen. When asked about it, she explained how she did not really think the ibuprofen would help, but it still kind of does. The belief in medication is present, but malleable. Her use of ibuprofen did not reflect negatively on her Christian Science belief; it just was not a simple yes or no answer when it came to belief. So, for all purposes of the word, it's better we understand belief as a fluid notion, rather than a solid one. A better way to picture the concept of belief is to imagine it as a pool: with a shallow end which dips into a deep end. Some people enjoy diving straight into the deep end, completely immersed in the waters of belief. But some prefer staying in less deep waters, or maybe they swim back and forth but never get their hair wet. And maybe there are others, sat on the side of the pool simply dipping their feet in.

What this means is that users are able to believe without believing. In other words, users can play with levels of belief without ever relinquishing the idea that what they are engaging with is fictional. Contrary to what people attacking whatever new media exists may say, audiences are able to distinguish between reality and fiction while still delving into a believable story and coming out the other side with their lives deeply affected. One does not need to believe in the historical accuracy of *Star Wars*, or even self-identify as a Jedi, for *Star Wars* to mean something significant to them.

It is not just horror which engages with the active play of belief in its audience. Wrestling audiences, for one, have always played with belief. The role of the storyline takes precedence, resulting in even anger from fans when the fourth wall is broken and feuding wrestlers are seen hanging out jovially with one another. The importance of this in-character communication in wrestling is even given its own term: kayfabe. The insistence is to continue to portray the narratives as genuine, despite how audiences know they are contrived. Similarly, role playing games such as Dungeons and Dragons insist on in-character storytelling, and blacklist "metagaming", or talking with knowledge of the game as frame for conversation. In other words, players should not make decisions based on the knowledge of the game and common game mechanics, but rather as their character truly would. Like supernatural gothic horror in the past, this is often seen as destructive to the individuals who play. Dungeons and Dragons itself has been blamed for violence in the past, particularly due to the player's supposed inability to distinguish the game from reality.

The engagement of playing with belief will be a recurring theme for us as we explore the variety of online horror stories that exist. The online environment lives within the context of belief play, and horror in particular thrives with it. Stories are often told with the framing of truth around it: some have hopes that it will eventually grow to be an urban legend through the sharing of the narratives, while others are simply happy for the narrative to live as the fiction with real framing. Regardless of initial intention, the trope is common and important to grasp in order to truly understand horror online, or even online storytelling more generally.

The Possibilities of Horror

Much of our introduction so far has drifted at times from the base horror genre to discussing Twitch Plays Pokémon and wrestling. It may seem strange to drift so much occasionally; however, it is important to realise the horror genre is not, at its core, considered or structured any differently than other genres. The intention to play with the belief of its audience is found in other genres but utilised in the horror genre for the purposes of a different emotional end. There are a few different elements to the horror genre worth considering.

The most cited is that the horror genre allows the audience to play with the direct reality of supernatural entities in a vastly different way than other genres. Other genres, such as fantasy, might include aspects of the supernatural reality, and even urban fantasy allows us to engage with supernatural entities in our current world. However, the horror genre presents a different approach to the supernatural – a horrific one. The presentation of these entities is often horrific and terrifying is interesting to explore in greater detail. For many supernatural horror narratives, their presence, even fictionally, is important. The most famous example of supernatural horror which often comes to people's mind is H P Lovecraft. Lovecraft coined the idea of "cosmic fear" – an instinctual feeling similar in both origin and feeling to a religious feeling, an instinctual inner sense of fear.

For Lovecraft, then, monsters are inherently possible because they are a part of us in the way we think. They are our instinctual fear, something so a part of us that they are a part of what makes us us. Monsters are inherently real – they are present in the thoughts and emotions of those who share it. Monsters are real through their effect, and their effect makes them inherently possible. It is a self-perpetuating cycle which constantly gives life to the world of monsters. This cycle has another benefit – it gradually breaks down the standing boundaries between reality and fiction.

This book will follow through an exploration of the inherent possibilities of digital monsters. All of them have a level of possibility, but there is a gradient of reality present; a slow increase in the amount of destruction to the perceived boundaries between reality and fiction. And all of them have an effect – a strong effect on the communities and cultures who tell them. This book not only explores monsters, but also explores their meanings and their impact. In essence, we will be exploring the possibilities and realities they possess. And we will see how monsters, especially digital monsters, are real.

Chapter 2
Massively Created Monsters

In 2009, a user on the Something Awful forum reflected on the thread's efforts to create a monster. Despite the fictional nature of the narratives, and everyone's knowledge of the combined endeavour of the narrative creation, there was still a sense of something greater happening that each individual had little grasp on. User rinksi wrote:

> But there is no person – not the people making photoshops, not his original creator, and not the guys making the Marble Hornets videos – who is solely in charge of this story anymore. He's growing organically from our combined feedback and contributions. He's the larger organism and we are his cells. We're simultaneously in control and not in control. For all intents and purposes, the Slender Man is a living entity.

This statement is a strong sentiment of the power of mass communal storytelling. The way various users feel connected to more than just the story, and more than just the community. It influences and impacts how they feel connected to the subject of the story itself. Despite the fictional nature of the narrative, the play with both the narrative and belief in the writings of the monsters, means the monsters created have their own life. They live and thrive in the boundary between the place of reality and the kingdom of the fictional. They live with the community, but also outside of the community. These monsters are ones who thrive in the place of the middle.

The two primary cases we will be exploring in this chapter are the Slender Man and The Rake. Both were created through the combined effort of many people in many places in the world, all thinking and contributing to the new life of a new monster. These monsters have altered life online, thriving far beyond typical years of online phenomena. But what exactly are these monsters doing to the environment there? What do they mean to the communities who first spun their tales, and continued their retellings a decade later?

The Slender Man

The Slender Man is found in a variety of cultures around the world. He is known as Fear Dubh, the Black Man, in Scotland, where he lingers in the forest and haunts lonely paths through the woodlands. In Germany, he is known as Der Großmann, or the Tall Man, where he prowls the Black Forest. Wherever he is, he leaves violence and terror in his wake. An all-too-thin and all-too-tall fairy who appears, at first glance, like a man in a suit, makes children disappear in the middle of the night. His mythology spread to the United States, where he took blame for missing children and mysterious fires which destroyed records of his presence.

Or, at least, that's how the stories go.

In 2009, the online community of the Something Awful forums gave birth to the Slender Man. Something Awful forum user Gerogerigege started a discussion thread for creating paranormal images in the summer of 2009. They claimed creating paranormal images had been a hobby of theirs and invited the forum community to "make a shit load." For the first two or three pages of the thread, the posts were varied; images and discussions arose on how best to make a photo realistic enough to fool the paranormal believing community, but vague enough to blend with photos in similar circles.

On the third page, the flow of discussion changed when user Victor Surge posted two of his photoshopped images, accompanied by short captions. His photos depicted a strange humanoid creature with too long of limbs and an eerie feel who lingered behind children – a creature he dubbed "The Slender Man". Very quickly, Victor Surge's images caused a shift in conversation. Other users, inspired by Victor Surge, began to post their own take on the Slender Man, and soon the forum thread, which was once dedicated to creating paranormal images in general, became a type of digital campfire where users swap harrowing tales and eerie images of the Slender Man. The tales took many forms – some retained the initial purpose of the thread and took the form of photoshopped images. Others wrote their narratives. The written accounts took two forms: some were personal tales in which users detailed a horrific encounter with the Slender Man, but more frequently, they took the form of pseudo-documents and fake reports from fictional academic texts, copies of classified emails, reprints of newspaper articles, and other formats in which writers utilised as formats of "proof".

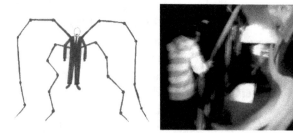

Figure 1: Two depictions of the Slender Man. Left by user genesplicer; right by Victor Surge

About halfway through the lifespan of the forum thread, one user, ce gars, began to post videos about the Slender Man, this time in the form of a web series. His YouTube channel, Marble Hornets, took a *Blair Witch*-style documentary-like approach, in which the user was uploading segments of a friend's unfinished film project which came to a mysterious stop. The series became immensely popular outside of the original audience of the Something Awful forum and brought the horror of the Slender Man to different areas of the internet.

Simultaneously, other storytelling forms around the Slender Man began to find a foothold online. Blogs such as Just Another Fool began, which were focused on their own storytelling formats. Entire websites of forums started to sprout with a location for Slender Man narratives to exist, and one, Slender Nation, even supported its own podcast.

A video game, called *Slender: the Eight Pages*, appeared after a few years. It was a short game in which the player had to collect eight pages scrawled with strange writing echoing a similar style of the writing of victims in Marble Hornets. It found quite a large amount of success, mostly due to the rise in popularity of Let's Plays – a form of online video in which video game players record themselves and their gameplay and upload this for others to watch. Its success led to Blue Isle Studios releasing another video game, *Slender: the Arrival*.

The Slender Man is perhaps one of the most popular creepypastas, especially regarding its recognition to those outside the creepypasta community through a variety of its forms. Along with creepypastas Jeff the Killer and smile.jpg, the Slender Man is one of the most prominent and is often the only one which those outside the community can recognise. Its prolific nature is somewhat due to its presence across many forms and locations online. However, it is difficult to tell if its popularity is due to this proliferation of narrative types, or if its proliferation is a side-effect of its popularity. Regardless, the Slender Man is an icon of creepypasta and horror in the digital age. His history is filled with communal re-creation and transformation.

The Slender Man first lurked in the background of photographs. From a distance, the Slender Man appears as a tall thin man wearing a suit. But when the viewer gets closer, the form changes. His height is inhumanly extraordinary. His suit sometimes stretches strangely, as if it is not a suit but a second skin. At times, he has appendages which sprout from his back – sometimes branch-like, sometimes insect-like, and even sometimes as tentacles. His face, typically lacking facial features, sometimes shifts as well – occasionally with too oddly proportioned, or just depicting a pair of glowing white eyes.

He often makes children disappear, with no mention of any violent acts. Violence, when displayed, is reserved for adults. But his *modus operandi* shifts as much as his appearance does. In some narratives, he attacks by impaling on tree branches, while in others his victims are disembowelled. In some, children are not the only victims who disappear, making adults vanish as well. In some narratives, the Slender Man is seen as being able to change a person's mind to work for him, as an almost mindless actor called a proxy.

As this description makes obvious, there is nothing clear or concise about the Slender Man. The multitude of "ifs" and "sometimes" that is necessary for any description of him demonstrates the multitudes of narratives which arise out of his creation and continued retellings. His appearance and actions shift from one story to another, all depending on the creativity of what the storyteller specifically wants. The result is a creature who spun out of control of the audience while also firmly in their hands. Each subsequent story both spread the narrative to new grounds as well as rooted its presence in the online world, both refusing ownership and allowing many to own him all at once. Even though Victor Surge incited the creations with his initial post, he never claimed to own the story or idea of the Slender Man. Each contribution feeds into the greater mythology, as the narrative is always greater than a single contribution.

One of the ways this truly took shape is hinted at it in the quote from rinski at the beginning of this chapter. Rinksi was responding to the creation of the Slender Man as they witnessed it happening; the way contributions fed a larger mythology rather than living and standing on their own. At some point in the forum's life, the word "tulpa" became associated with the Slender Man, giving credence to a whole new mythological theory for the Slender Man's life: the Tulpa Theory.

A tulpa, as understood by the community, is said to have its roots in Tibetan Buddhism, though these links are tangential at best. It is most connected to the Western esoteric religious movement Theosophy, and Theosophists have been the ones to paint the connection to Buddhism, even though it never really appears in separate Buddhist texts. Theosophy made popular the use of affirmations to better oneself, in which the power of thought is brought to greater power and presence through the force of consistent and massive thought. For affirmations, this occurs with a repetition of phrases which then impact the outside world. For example, saying "I will have a good day" several times in the morning while looking in the mirror will manifest into you having a good day. Tulpas are much more powerful versions of this. The force of thought is not just to embody an emotional experience, such as having a good day, but to bring into being a true physical entity.

The first recorded instance of a tulpa was from Theosophist

Alexandra David-Néel, who claimed to learn of this from Buddhists she was living with in Tibet. After her publication, others followed her record of thought-forms, and referenced them as their primary source of information on the topic. Further details of tulpas is found in Annie Besant and Charles Leadbetter's book *Thought-Forms*, published in 1925. In David-Néel's account of tulpas, she described how they can grow to become too powerful for the creator to control any longer. These now loose thoughtforms can become havoc to society and the one who once created it.

If tulpas gain strength and power from engagement of thought, it is easy to see how the Slender Man can begin to retain the horror: with so many people, in so many locations of the world, all thinking about and contributing their ideas to the Slender Man, the power of his existence can be intensely large. He may have once been fictional, but the power of the thoughts contributing to him has caused his existence to take shape. Like the quote from rinksi at the beginning, all the contributions and narratives feed an organism they have no control over, as he grows and manifests due to these contributions.

Even though no community member creating Slender Man narratives truly bought into the idea that the Slender Man is truly manifest somewhere out there in this world, the Tulpa Theory brought forward the true conception of what the mythology was actually doing as it was being created, with each individual feeling both connected to, and inherently disconnected from, the individual monster they created.

The Rake

The Rake started in 2005 and/or 2006 on 4chan in a similar way to the call on the Something Awful forum which led to the Slender Man. An anonymous poster created a thread with the call "Let's create a new monster" (in a title incredibly similar to the "create paranormal images" which gave birth to the Slender Man). There were many ideas circulated, but a combination of a couple different ideas led to the creation of The Rake. As opposed to the Slender Man, who grew organically from an initial post, The Rake started with intention, and the compiling of elements which are relevant to a truly scary new monster.

The community decided upon several features which were particularly prevalent: tall, about six feet in height; humanoid; skin that is pale and grey in colour; no nose; a mouth that is only slightly visible, but then opens large on a hinge; eats meat; looks human enough to be able to disguise itself with a fedora and trench coat. This list was amended to have eyes only slightly larger than human, to obscure its diet, and to ignore the amount of human to be easily disguised. It became a strange creature, humanoid but hunched and animal-like in action.

Reposts of The Rake's story began appearing on LiveJournal only a year or so later. It spread through various forum websites, from 4chan to the Something Awful forum. In August of 2010, the story was posted to reddit. On December of that year, a single topic blog on Tumblr was launched, centralising the stories of The Rake, compiling them as "sightings" as well as fanart. An altered YouTube video with a monster (actually taken from the video game *Resistance 3*) became related to The Rake directly, only helping to spread the narrative even more. Something Awful user Brian Somerville brought The Rake narratives to his own blog, which was later quoted and repeated on the Something Awful forum in 2009, on the same thread giving birth to the Slender Man.

The story goes that The Rake has been around for many hundred years. The narrative compiles different "archives" of various accounts of The Rake throughout the years, the earliest being a log from 1691, and the most detailed from 2006. As the introduction to the collection details, there was a compilation of over two dozen documents spanning that length of time and four continents. The stories are all slightly varied, with different levels of information given on The Rake, but with a connecting piece of the power and fear of his voice. The longest narrative is narrated by a woman who details an account of The Rake. She woke to find "at the foot of the bed, sitting and facing away from us, there was what appeared to be a naked man, or a large hairless dog of some sort. Its body position was disturbing and unnatural, as if it had been hit by a car or something." The creature moved and said something to her husband, before turning and running to her daughter's room and attacking the girl. Both the husband and daughter died in a car crash that night, while rushing to the hospital. The woman then sought to assemble information on The Rake from a variety of other people (the rest of the collected materials).

Seeing The Rake automatically changes a person. The Rake's appearance and voice is what shifts people. Hearing the voice, or even seeing him, moves someone from a life once lived in ignorance to a place of being Transformed by the event. They are part of society, moving and living in the everyday moments, but are forever seeking answers to their inherent questions. The woman who compiles the narratives is doing so in order to seek answers to her own Transformation.

The Monstrous Audience

The Slender Man and The Rake are both from similar backgrounds, built following similar avenues. The two were constructed by a community's collective effort. Even though the narratives themselves differ, and the monsters look different, they share similarities in how they are appropriated and understood by the community. There are two main elements that are present in the narrative of both the Slender Man and The Rake: facelessness and powerlessness.

The Slender Man is easily associated with the concept of being faceless due to how he often lacks a face. The faceless monster has been lingering in the fearful corners of humans' minds for some time. He echoes the idea of Lovecraft's "cosmic fear" – a concept that there is a grand fear inherent in the human experience we just cannot comprehend. Lovecraft's monsters in his Cthulhu Mythos are comprised of older beings which humans have no capacity to comprehend. The Ancient Ones, as they are called, are unknowable. Lovecraft's "cosmic fear" is an instinctual feeling similar to a religious feeling.

The inspiration of Lovecraft's "cosmic fear" has not left horror after Lovecraft; it has laid the foundation of horror storytelling, and its historical traces through the horror genre has continued. Lovecraft's "cosmic fear" puts the reader in a position of fearful interaction with the Supernatural Other. The Slender Man and The Rake inhabit this strange unknowable form.

As the stories about the Slender Man continued on the Something Awful forums, an important question regarding his constantly altered nature arose: what makes a Slender Man story a Slender Man story? The community's answer was to not set any definitive canon, asserting that every narrative is considered canonical to the Slender Man. So, his shifting nature became canonical to his understanding.

The Slender Man became defined by that which could not be defined. The Slender Man became known for his inconsistent nature. By allowing each writer or artist's view of the Slender Man to stand as authoritative and accurate, the Slender Man himself shifted in understanding to one which is, in effect, constantly changing. Something Awful forum user cloudy described the Slender Man in a short narrative as having "several consistent identifying markers, with other traits changing or 'transforming' from image to image." This is a narrativised account of what we have already seen – how sometimes the appendages are present and sometimes not, and how his actions alter so drastically from story to story. User Chaos Hippy wrote: "You don't understand. You don't understand! He's not transforming or coming out of his shell. What we see is changing as we're exposed to something we should never see," Perhaps most succinctly clarified by the Riffie, the ever-changing Slender Man is quite simply "beyond our comprehension."

Similarly, The Rake moves and acts with some unknowable purpose. The victims he chooses are seemingly random, as is his movements to get in and out of houses without the victims' knowledge. His voice is quiet but deadly. It is the voice of The Rake, and the name it speaks, which causes violence. The voice itself is a secret, only given to those who are unlucky enough to hear it. Knowing more about The Rake only puts characters more into a position of uncertainty and fear. The more accumulated knowledge, the more its actually damaging or frightening. So the Slender Man and The Rake are both faceless in their understanding.

But facelessness is not limited to the monsters themselves. Characters in the narratives on the Slender Man and on The Rake are always in a stage of transition. For the Slender

Man, most characters began as those like everyone else – a normal member of society. However, their interaction with the Slender Man changes them. They become removed from society by a fraction. In a mocked newspaper article, a young girl saw their sister being taken by a Slender Man, but she is not believed and actively ignored. In an account acting as a psychologist's report on children whose classmate was taken in the woods, their account and description of the Slender Man is equally as discounted. Their relationship with the monster removes them from an active part of a trustworthy society, though they are not as removed as those the Slender Man has taken.

Massively created monsters are a communal act of storytelling. Many online narratives are told using in-character communication. Essentially, users assert the truth and veracity of the narratives they share without ceding their position as author or audience member. The best example of this type of storytelling is detailed in the horror sub-reddit No Sleep, where a rule for posting and commenting states that "everything is true here even if it isn't" (see Chapter 5). Those with narratives would claim they "found" the documents, emails or photographs and are sharing these finds with the online community. Some are more performative in nature, including one from Victor Surge, where they posit an on-going experience, or that while reading the stories on the forum thread they can hear Slender Man's characteristic tapping at their window.

The interactivity of in-character communication encourages transformation of the text, whether by act of author or audience. The storytelling remains communal, despite individual creators arising. This is echoed in the Slender Man's Tulpa Theory. The Tulpa Theory is one discussed purely in play, but the concept underlying demonstrates the way in which individual creativity could flourish under one larger mythos. Each individual author is allowed to have their personal interpretation shine as canonical.

Despite this, in-character communication highlights the force the community holds above the individual. While the author may hold creative licence, the authority of authorship is often non-existent within the context of in-character communication – the ultimate authority is given to the community rather than the individual. The original poster of the Slender Man, Victor Surge, never corrected or claimed the Slender Man narrative as his own intellectual property. The Slender Man is, and always has been, communal property. This is how mass communal storytelling works.

In-character communication demonstrates the way in which facelessness is not only reserved for the Slender Man and The Rake but are also put onto the audience. The act of writing itself is a faceless one. The author's work is shared separate from author, becoming part of the communal narrative itself. This also echoes the experience of the characters in these narratives: they become faceless to society. And as they faceless, they are also powerless. As both characters and audiences become faceless, they lose the individual power they had – becoming less so until they are fully removed, or taken, from society.

At the heart of all of this is alterations to the categorical understandings of self and society through the full interaction with the monster. The characters and audience members start in a category of those who have been unaffected – who live a normal life. Upon interaction with the monster, they are forcibly moved to the outskirts of this category, almost a full other one. This one is full of those ignored and silenced; those removed from social consideration, but not so removed as to be completely gone. They are suddenly placed in a category that sits between two more firmly categories: those present, and those gone. They are present but gone in consideration and thought.

Importantly, it is not the individuals who have agency over this alteration of understanding and social placement, but the monster. The characters who are in the process of transitioning, or already have, have no agency in their own progression and changing of status. This agency is instead given over to the secondary and supernatural force of the monster. The facelessness they are feeling is inherent in their new categorical position and is a result of the actions of another.

The powerlessness of the characters is also extended to the audience in a similar way in how the audience was impacted by facelessness. The visual narratives, such as the digitally manipulated images of the Slender Man or the YouTube video of The Rake, have a sense of control instilled in them. This control is kept away from the audience, who is forced to view only what has been presented to them. A well-made image will not have much evidence of its alteration, even to a well-trained viewer.

But powerlessness also extends to the audience in the actual narrative. The Tulpa Theory demonstrates how the process and idea of creating an online urban legend has the consequence of releasing authorial control. The author cannot retain connection to the story for it to truly live elsewhere. Even when the narrative carries a strong knowledge of the realm of fiction, the push for realistic horror and realistic understandings of how the flow of information occurs means author connection is forfeited. Often, the writing of mass communal narratives meant that authorial connection was not even expected. Writers wrote to contribute to a greater narrative, rather than to gain some kind of respect as writer or artist.

To recall the quote by forum user rinski cited at the

beginning of this chapter, authors themselves felt power-less in their own authorial construction. Victor Surge, the user who first crafted the Slender Man, has renounced all authorial claim over the Slender Man, and has since his first posting. The Slender Man belongs to no one. The Rake exists outside of the individuals who first crafted his image through meticulous formulations of the monstrous image. Whether they truly exist in the world as a physical mani-festation, like a tulpa, is truly unimportant – they are still tulpas who thrive through the words and images crafted by people who no longer have control over the creation they have spun.

Playing with Monsters

In our introductory chapter, we discussed the various roles of belief and play with belief that is possible in the world of digital monsters. For those massively created monsters, the role of play is heavily present, but as a quiet presence which rules over the background of its existence. If we are to ask questions about the role of belief of the writers, we would largely be missing the point of these monsters and their role for both story and community.

The play with belief in these narratives has been largely misunderstood by those outside. Quite a few studies and explorations into the Slender Man begin their look at the 2014 Wisconsin stabbings in the United States, where two twelve-year-old girls stabbed a third friend of theirs and left her for dead in the name of the Slender Man. For many outside the creepypasta community, this stabbing was their first introduction to the Slender Man and the world of horror writing he represents. A proverbial witch-hunt began. People who authored Slender Man narratives online were blamed for the stabbing. Many media outlets began to call the attack "The Slender Man Stabbing", removing agency from the stabbers to the strange monstrous creature. One blogger wrote that "There is something really sick and twisted about the people who put up websites like this."

This blame shift to the community is unnecessary and misses many points, not the least of which is the role of violence and mental health in the outside world (ignoring the role these play in the narratives themselves). The result is a maintenance of blame where it fully does not belong. If the community itself rejects these acts (which they do), then why focus at all on these attacks? In many ways, the media centring on these kinds of acts and blaming the narratives themselves for it, echoes the previous attacks on popular culture, such as rock and roll and the contemporary attack on video games.

The play of belief happening with the Slender Man and The Rake is purely in a playful process of storytelling action. Like our original poster on the Something Awful forum which gave birth to the thread of the Slender Man, the fooling of individuals to believe in its reality is only a fun side-effect, but not the true nature of it. The point is the actual act of creation itself. Each in-character conversation is with a smile and wink, rather than with a sincerity to fool. A good comparison here would be with *the Blair Witch Project*. While some may have been fooled, most were not. The movie was not created with the intention to fool, but with the intention to simply have a good narrative with a sense of reality. The fun is in the joyful play of "what if", rather than a full sense of "yes". Like children who, at a sleepover, run into a bathroom to say Bloody Mary – most know that nothing will happen, but the reality of the way the narratives are told leaves a sense of wonder and anticipation.

Instead of thinking of the Slender Man and The Rake as being told with hidden giggles to fool, it is best to think of these narratives as being told over a digital campfire. These are simply contemporary and online versions of the type of narratives you would hear while cuddling a mug of hot chocolate and staring at the crackling flames. The realism causes the heart to pound a little faster. But when you leave the campfire, packed up the tent, and gone home, the pounding is gone and the narrative only lingers as a fun story that entertained you on a clear and cold night. The play with reality and belief is fun, but mostly as a way through which the narrative can truly thrive, rather than an engagement to fool or trick. Beyond that, most participating with the narrative are in on the level of reality, and know the story to be fictional, but a fun story to tell around a digital campfire.

Massive Communal Effects

In our introductory chapter, we have thought about how monsters exist in the effect they have on society. But what are the effects the Slender Man and The Rake are having on the community that creates and retells their stories?

The digital community which gave birth to the Slender Man and The Rake are the creepypasta community. The term "creepypasta" came from "copypasta" – used in early stages of online communication when it was necessary to copy the words and paste it elsewhere in order to share. The horror variants of these widely shared narratives became dubbed "creepypastas". The ultimate goal of creepypastas is to be shared outside from authorial name. In essence, the aim of a creepypasta is to be become an online urban legend. Whether or not this has already been successful is a conversation for a later chapter. The main point of the community for our consideration here is that it remains faceless.

The communally created monsters' lack of existence in the social categories they control demonstrates a key aspect of the monstrous – that a monster demonstrates a crisis in our cultural and social categories. The Slender Man and The Rake disrupt the culture of their community through their existence and disrupt the lives of the characters through their actions.

If we remove the overarching scary monsters with some different outside force, our previously detailed understandings of the world do not really change. The monsters provide a larger metaphor for the community to express dissent with the issues of larger, typically Western, social norms. The monsters are a physical expression of the social forces of the nonvirtual outside world. For example, the narratives demonstrate a commentary on the views of those with mental health issues in wider society: those who are marginalised and suffer because of it. Those who are affected are often considered as insane, resulting in their testimonies being silenced.

The anxiety of this middle category also, in many ways, expresses how the authors view their own digital selves. If we change our understanding of the social categories to reflect the various levels of physical to virtual, we see something interesting. The normal world that exists before the monster intervened will be the physical world, the purely non-digital world. Those completely removed by the monsters is the completely virtual, i.e. not present physically. The user finds themselves in a strange middle ground between the two. In 2009 and 2010, when these stories were at an intense height, the concept of an online community and a virtual home was not as readily found nor as commonly accepted, though the concept is still often met with much question.

Some of the language used online reflect the dichotomy between virtual and physical, including the designation of "IRL" or "in real life" – essentially leaving the virtual environment as the one which is not "real". This means that any substantial relationship or connection made online lies somewhere in between what is real and what is not real – a strange mediatory category in which their full online experience exists. This can provide a great sense of anxiety for the individual members of the online environment.

The monsters this community created reflects their own anxieties and concerns, while demonstrating the monstrous presence of outside forces on their own social considerations. They are not considered fully present, their testimonials of love and acceptance in a digital location silenced and ignored. They are the victims of the monsters, though in this case the monsters are the non-digital forces which have determined what reality can consist of, and forces this onto the lives of others. The monsters are the outside forces, the media outlets that condemned the community purely for telling stories, or the family and friends who, even while being pleasant in intent, tell those who occasionally live in digital environments that their relationships and locations are not real. The voices which determine these avenues are not possible are the voices of The Rake, whispering death and uncertainty in the ear of its victims, or are the sound of the tapping Slender Man at your window.

Chapter 3:
Virtual Monsters and Monstrous Video Games

It is a bit strange to have a separate chapter entitled the virtual in a book describing things that are digital. Digital and virtual monsters seem to be pretty similar, and apart from some pedantic academics who like to overly define most words people regularly use, it's not too far from the truth. But virtual monsters, and by this I mean monsters that are of the virtual itself, may be different than the monsters we've looked at so far. Some of the digital monsters we have explored are new monsters which have been created in a digital environment. They tell us ideas about the digital communities which tell them, and the people who retell them. They teach us about what matters to us in our new environments – what is scary now.

But what about monsters which do not mimic the fairies of old like the Slender Man? Or strange inhuman monsters like The Rake? Or ones that are not mysteriously realistic like those on No Sleep (to be explored in a later chapter)? What happens when the monstrosity we explore in the digital world is the digital itself? What happens when the virtual becomes a monster?

These stories are about the virtual as monstrous. For many of these monsters, the virtual world is no longer just the location these monsters take shape, rather they take the virtual worlds and mould them into something monstrous. No longer is the internet the place where people meet in order to create the monsters; the internet here has become the monster itself.

Ben Drowned

In 2000, Nintendo released the *Legend of Zelda: Majora's Mask* on their Nintendo 64 home consoles. *Majora's Mask* stood, and still does stand, as a stark contrast to the normal format of Zelda games. Following both *Link to the Past* (1991) and *Ocarina of Time* (1998), Nintendo had begun to establish a system which would stand for several decades in the *Legend of Zelda* series. The games are strictly narrated, with little wiggle room for the player to follow their own course. The player is led to a variety of dungeons, or temples, in which they solve puzzles, often gain a particular weapon, and use that weapon to defeat the boss of that temple. And then the process continues a set number of times, until the player faces the final boss.

Majora's Mask (2000), on the other hand, is different for several reasons. The most obvious is how the developers had a very short time for development. Because of this, *Majora's Mask* uses the same engine, graphics, and character models from *Ocarina of Time*. The world is also a little smaller, with only four different main regions, each with its own temple, for the player to battle through. One of the primary differences with *Majora's Mask*, however, is the introduction of a timer to the game. The whole game must be completed in three in-game days. A clock is introduced to the interface, and players are constantly reminded of how much time is left if players play a particular song, the game clock, and many other elements, reset.

This clock, as well as some of the background narrative of the game, is what makes *Majora's Mask* stand out as rather different game to the rest, and a rather dark game. The game takes place immediately after the events of *Ocarina of Time*. An imp from the woods, called Skull Kid, has stolen a magical mask from the Happy Mask Salesman, a mask said to harbour a dark power. The Happy Mask Salesman enlists our main playable character Link to get the mask back. The game must be completed in three game days from this request, as Skull Kid is planning to crash the moon into the town in three days.

Because the player is essentially repeatedly replaying the same three days, the player learns the schedules of the various townsfolk, and can solve many of their problems throughout the course of the three days. This is in combination with completing the four temples in the four various areas – the guardians there, once freed, can come to help stop the moon from falling. Even though many steps are taken to solve the city's problems, and many people and areas are helped, at the end of the solution, the player must reset time, and all help provided is suddenly reset. The world reverts to how it was at the beginning of the three days. The player only keeps the reward item, and everyone and everything returns to the beginning one more time.

The reuse of character models, the continuous replaying of days and the darkness of the narrative of the moon falling, all lead to a darker version of a familiar game. Masks are acquired in the game which cause the main character to change shape, but the transformation sequence played is one of utter terror and pain. The whole mood led to a popular fan theory that Link died, and the game is playing out a version of purgatory in a nightmare-esque world.

Majora's Mask's inherent creepiness paved the way for an understanding of the virtual monstrous in the form of the popular creepypasta called Ben Drowned. The horror narrative follows a haunted Nintendo 64 cartridge of *Majora's Mask*. The game is glitched beyond a recognisable old glitched game, and with a fear and creepiness which makes it appear as if something greater is occurring. The previous owner of the game, Ben, was a young man who died in a drowning accident, and the game at first seems to be haunted by him. As the narrator delves further into the questions of the game, something even stranger is occurring.

The narrative of Ben Drowned started with an online user named Jadusable posting on multiple online forums in 2010 about his finding of a weirdly glitched cartridge. He uploaded on his YouTube page videos of his various attempts to play the game. In each attempt, something weird would be occurring, such as Link bent strangely, or a statue randomly appearing behind him every couple seconds. The music is also altered. Instead of the music which typically plays in the game, a version of "The Song of Healing" plays in reverse. In town, all non-playable characters were gone which gave Jaduable a growing sense of loneliness.

Figure 2: Screenshot from Ben Drowned video

Most of the text for the first two videos are either garbled, as in the image, or segments of written text from different points in the game. The last two videos change this, so the dialogue boxes become changed to attempt conversation. Strange sound affects also occur, including the Happy Mask Salesman's laughter and the Skull Kid's laughter.

As Jedusable continues to explore the supposedly haunted game, he begins to find that the game itself is the monster. There is no haunted ghost which trips up the video game – it is some monster in the machine that manipulates Jedusable, to the point of him having trouble sleeping and pulling himself away from most social interactions. He describes feeling his sanity slowly slip away.

Smile.jpg

The initial start of smile.jpg is unknown but is mostly tied to the forum site 4chan. The story revolves around a singular image of a dog, resembling a Siberian Husky, with a strange humanlike smile. The image is said to drive its viewers insane. At some point in its history, a story became attached to the image, the story of Mr. L, who goes in search of more information on the "cyber-legend" of the image smile.jpg.

The written story of smile.jpg follows a "Mr. L" who goes in search of more information on the smile.jpg image, as the picture is only occasionally seen in various places online, and few others have described ever seeing it. He finds a "Mary E." who encountered the image on a bulletin board system for her neighbourhood. The conversation with her is strange. She remains in a different room and he never sees her – they communication only through a door while her husband attempts to calm her. In further attempts to find out more, Mr. L reaches out for more information on a variety of websites. Mary E then sends an email, pleading for him to stop, describing the image as something which gets in your head, haunts your dreams, and pleads for you to "spread the word" and share the pain with another. She almost immediately after commits suicide. Mr. L then receives an email with an attachment, describing it as giving information and "spreading the word". The end of the story has an image of an oddly human-like smile on a dog, lit only by the flash of a polaroid camera. Most interesting is how, near the end of the narrative, a floppy disk with the image on it is burned and said to have screamed as it was destroyed.

Figure 3: Smile.jpg

Lavender Town Syndrome

In 1996, the games *Pokémon Red* and *Pokémon Green* were released in Japan. These were some of the first Pokémon games. The game leads the player to explore different areas of the geography of the region Kanto, starting in Palette Town, and moving through the world, catching Pokémon and battling trainers.

One of these towns, Lavender Town, is known for a creepy town. It is a small area, most notable for a large tower. Pokémon Tower is a large building of Pokémon graves. Weaving through the building, the player encounters ghosts and shamans, always filled with the soft sound of strange and eerie music. The town itself is tinted slightly purple, only continuing to instil an odd feel to the players. Like Ben Drowned, the creepy and eerie atmosphere of a game lent itself to the creation of a virtual monster.

The background music in Lavender Town is so eerie and unsettling it became a large interest for fans of the game. The song combines sharp and high-pitched synthesised sounds with jarring discordant chords, combined to feel more than a little frightening. Apart from the monster embedded in the idea of Lavender Town, the music present in the game is quite frankly dreadful, in the true sense of the word: it is full of a sense of dread.

The story goes that there was a string of suicides in Japan, about 200 children killed themselves, just after the release of the Pokémon game in 1996. Other children suffered severe migraines or nosebleeds. Some turned violent when parents tried to take the game away from them. Others cried until they vomited. All the affected children had stopped playing after reaching Lavender Town.

The developers, Game Freak, tried to cover up the deaths and resultant erratic behaviour. They recalled first editions of the game, and later releases had replaced the music with a new version which did not drive children insane. They were successful until an employee leaked their report on Lavender Town Syndrome, including some of the symptoms of the victims.

Users began to add more elements to the story to make it appear more realistic, including details about Kyoto corporate disclosure laws, and including made-up names of employees and child victims. Some ran the audio through a spectrograph, which generates a visual map of audio frequencies which, when they did, resulted in a picture the in-game sprite of a Lavender Town ghost. Some have the image of the ghost accompanied with the message "leave now" spelled out.

The collective evidence, combined with the reality that children actually can hear tones too high for adult hearing, made some people truly believe the story as real. Some of the easiness to believe comes from how the music truly is a bit creepy. Some places, and even people who were children once playing the games themselves, swear the music does cause headaches. The idea that there are supernatural things children can see but adults cannot is a popular horror trope and one that's also present in many different cultures around the world, including Japan. This makes things a bit tricky when picking out the fact from the fiction in the case of the Lavender Town Syndrome.

That is, if we want or even care about picking out the differences. It is well established the idea that there were 200 suicides of children in Japan in the late 90s is a fabrication for the fun of the story, but the insistence that the original music has been changed for world release, as well as how the original music causes headaches, is still sometimes asserted, with even personal anecdotes of it being the case for them.

The Reality of the Virtual Monsters

This chapter demonstrated a shift in the type of monster on display. In our previous chapter, monsters were obviously supernatural creatures that have impeded our world and altered our understanding of our place within this world. They changed our placement in society by altering our understandings – placing us in a state of constant unknowing. The monsters in this chapter all share similar traits. In these cases, the virtual itself, the digital environment itself, is the monster. It is no longer some creepy tall fairy who steals children. It is the video games which are haunted, or whose music haunts your mind. The virtual is full of life and agency where there is no life and agency normally. For the Curious Case of the Smiling Dog, the image itself is somewhat alive – it talks to its audience and lives within the drives holding it, hissing when its burnt. Ben Drowned has a video game cartridge which thrives outside of the way a typical gaming cartridge thrives. It moves, lives and talks through the game. Lavender Town's music has a life of its own, an evil presence which sends hidden messages to children.

The fact the virtual environment itself is the monster is interesting. In our previous chapter, we saw how the internet provides an avenue through which monsters can be created. The Slender Man and The Rake were created as monsters of the human imagination, the human imagination was simply channelled through the medium of the internet. The image of the smiling dog is only a monster due to the internet itself. It is the virtual environment that the monster lives in. The Slender Man could exist outside of the internet, but these monsters rely on the online and the virtual to exist in order for their stories to even be understood. The story of the Lavender Town Syndrome and Ben Drowned need the base of the video game in order to grow and develop, and this growth creates the monster.

It is easy for these monsters to be monstrous and fearful because the virtual itself crosses once solid categories of real and fictional – put more simply the distinction between real and not-real. Our social category of real typically has several other characteristics, typically that which is physically present, something we have evidence of and can look at closely. We can point at it, as a thing that exists, and say "this thing is real." Even emotions, as things which are intangible, are only considered real when associated with an object or person we can see, and we can touch. We have taken advantage of the concept of real. And it makes it easy to claim when something is not real: I can't touch it, and it's not associated with someone I can touch, therefore it's not real.

The digital complicates things. The internet is real. It has real people who are interacting through this thing. But it's not something we can touch or we can see. And even though we are talking to these real people, we still can't touch them or see them. They are simply words on a screen associated with the rational knowledge of someone else being on the other side, but without any proof or evidence of this. A typical phrasing on the internet is "IRL" or "in real life", which contributes to this understanding – the way I am online is considered unreal in comparison to how I am when the screen is off. The online world is unreal, because it is always set in contrast to the offline, which has already been deemed as the place of the real.

As we mentioned in the first chapter, the digital world is in many ways real. The reality of the world is still present: in the conversations had, the emotions felt, and the education and crimes which can be committed there. To think of the online sphere as inherently different than the offline sphere is not only a misstep in rationality, but also a radical shift in either the understanding of the online world or even the offline world.

The internet and the virtual world we sometimes enjoy dwelling in is an environment which shifts the familiar in a way that is unfamiliar, while still being the bit we acknowledge and understand. The monsters we have looked at in this chapter are the same: they take the form in something familiar but twist it into something truly unfamiliar. The fear always starts with something innocuous, something familiar and normal. It's something we would not think about as harmful or scary or different. It's a video game or an online image. It is normal. But as the story progresses, the unfamiliar shows itself. The communication online is familiar, echoing normal human interaction, but in an unfamiliar environment. Video games are normal stories, normal images, twisted to the unfamiliar through the need for interaction.

Not only are the narratives explored here a demonstration of the monstrous, but the virtual is also a monster due to the twisting of the familiar to the unfamiliar. These representations of the monstrous are not new with the creepypastas on the virtual. Noël Carroll, a philosopher of horror, defines the monster as that which is a fusion both in a physical and a categorical way. The monster embodies two aspects which cannot happen at once happening at once. The vampire is both living and dead at the same time. The werewolf is both man and animal at the same time. Anthropologist Mary Douglas explored the concept of the monstrous pig in Israeli food laws, seeing it as monstrous in its crossing of categories of that which chews the cud and that which has cloven hooves. The monstrous, and the grotesque, is a concept which either occupies multiple categories when that is unjustified culturally speaking or falls between categories and are thus not accommodated in the cultural structure of thought. Anthropologist Edmund Leach described these things outside of categories as "non-things" because they fall between the understandings of social categories of things and considerations of thoughts.

So the digital world, a placement of reality where reality was not originally conceived to be, is a monster itself. And this becomes compounded when the virtual environment creates an environment of fear and creepiness. It feeds into the concept that these things can actually be the cultural monsters we already conceive of them to be. It becomes easy to think of a video game as being capable of driving children insane through its music. It becomes easy to think of a scary image which can somehow get into our system and corrupt us from the screen out.

The Possibilities of Virtual Monsters

It's no accident the Slender Man is known for lingering in the woods, nor that many monsters of folklore and urban legends find refuge in the forests. Forests are areas of wildness and danger, a place of the unknown. In the Germanic folklore recorded by the Brothers Grimm, the forest was a place of great transformation – society's conventions do not hold in the wilderness. Other great monsters are known to inhabit the deep sea. Lovecraft's Ancient Ones dwell in the deepest of the seas – the depth of the environment and the unknown it represents causes a level of madness to those who attempt to understand the deepest levels of that which is truly unknowable to the great depths of the sea. The wilderness and the sea are both places of danger and the undiscovered, making the possibilities of the monsters lingering there as inherently possible.

Being places in between, the wilderness and the sea are between categories. The forest as the place for transformation occurs because it is between – therefore transitional states of between are perfect for this type of location. The wilderness is akin to a monster, then. The deep sea is a monster. They are both location monsters that can create a monster through the possibilities such locations create.

The fact the online and the virtual is, itself, a monster,

means the possibilities of the monsters who dwell in the virtual are inherently more possible. Even though the monster of the community narratives were created with the intention of possibility in them, the retellings of the story of the Slender Man and The Rake were always with the knowledge the narrative sharing is a fun storytelling experiment. Even when telling with perceived sincerity, there is a quiet and underlying wink – everyone was in on the joke and the fiction.

Some of the narratives here are not so obviously fictional. The Lavender Town Syndrome is the best example of this. In the retellings of the music of Pokémon's story, some elements of the narrative are carried forward even when others are considered only part of a fabricated narrative. Part of the story about the Lavender Syndrome is the alteration of the music from the first run of the game, and the later publications, chalked up to the suicides about the Lavender Town music. Even for those who tell the narrative with the knowledge of the fabrication, some elements still hold on. Some YouTube videos have posted the "original" Japanese music from the first release, with others claiming that it caused headaches due to the pitch and music. Some of these even talk about the suicides being an obvious false claim perpetuated by the change in the music and the fact it causes headaches. The music has not altered, though. You can even listen to the claimed "original" simultaneously with the claimed "altered" music, and the music is exactly the same. There is something which is held as partially true and believable. The suicides were a step into the fictional, but the other smaller, and more believable, aspects of the narrative are still held on as true.

Ben Drowned also holds onto a certain aspect of the realities possible, even if the larger narrative can be more easily rejected. A glitched video game is very easily believable. So much so that the glitches are sometimes believed over the story of the haunted cartridge.

It is important to comment that there is still a level of fun and game that is being had. These narratives exist on a middle ground within the middle ground. Our previous narratives enjoyed the game of "what if" – we compared the feeling of connection to the horror with sitting around a campfire or enjoying games of daring while at a sleepover. No one trusted in full reality of the narratives, but the game and fun were in making a narrative as realistic as possible, though it never crossed into a true urban legend that lived on its own. The narratives here are a step closer to this possibility. Here, the realistic touches to the narrative have become so realistic they can linger on their own, even aside from the rest of the narrative. The fun is still present by putting together enough of a realistic narrative to live on its own, but the elements of reality are so believed it almost makes the rest of the narrative even less believable. We can believe in a creepily glitched video game cartridge, but maybe less in the growth the narrative takes when the video game becomes more sentient. We can believe in the music that is so creepy and high pitched it causes headaches, but maybe not to the point of the abundance of suicides.

The Curious Case of the Smiling Dog is the only one which does not have a more realistic counterpart. But it does draw on the virtual engagement of email chains, and an inherent fear within the system of email chains. Email forwardables were a common occurrence in early stages of online communication but were not completely new with the advent of the internet. Jan Brunvard has recorded instances of forwardables in the form of handwritten mail, most notably his collection of the "Red Velvet Cake". This story is about the sharing of a recipe for Red Velvet Cake, which supposedly came from the Waldorf Astoria Hotel.

The story goes that a woman, after having the cake at the hotel, request the recipe in a letter. The response comes back but with a bill for a sizable amount of money (which varies with each story). The woman decides to circulate the recipe as a form of revenge on the hotel which charged her for the recipe. The recipe, and the story accompanying it, was circulated, sometimes handwritten, sometimes simply shared, and even appeared in newspapers.

The email forwardable, then, is not so different than other forms of storytelling which occurred prior to the inception of the internet. The popularity of forwardables became so excessive that users were often inundated with large amounts of forwardable mail, to the point it rivalled the infamous spam mail. Some were related to anti-virus programs, wanting the narrative to be shared through a variety of forwarded messages. Some people share these because they find, if it is a humorous one, to be funny enough to share, while some share from a genuine, if sometimes misguided, attempt to contribute a solution to some given problem. The format of the email forwardable, therefore, was one which would be familiar for the audience of the smile.jpg image.

And the feared image in the form of an email forwardable takes the familiarity of the email forwarding system and moves it to an unfamiliar place. The email forwardable was already full of questionable pieces, including hidden viruses. The idea of a scary image hidden within that, one which would get into your brain and alter your life is still fearful.

These narratives are an interesting halfway point in our readings of narratives. They bridge the gap between legends online which are truly fictional, and legends online which are often considered possibly true. These stand between – they demonstrate the potentials and the possible monsters, without delving too far into the realm of reality.

The Effects of the Virtual

Regardless of their possibilities and potentialities, these monsters are still real to the community in the effects they have. So what are the effects of the digital monsters that turn the virtual itself into its own monstrous landscape?

These narratives are still fully part of the creepypasta community, being spread through the community, and sometimes arising from it in small snippets of possibility. With their position in the creepypasta community, the community tells the narrative without much connection to author. The intention to create something fully and wholly other than author, something that is as alive and has just as much agency as the monsters in the narratives.

Because of that, there are some connections and similarities in the effect of these monsters to those who have looked at previously. The primary element of noted difference for these monsters, as opposed to others, is the alterations of the online environment as, itself, a monster. The shifting causes an element of possibility which extends beyond the narratives of the others. Suddenly the tulpas created from the imagination of creators has a monstrous landscape to thrive in as well.

But these monsters not only make the digital environment the monster, it also shift the nature of the audience member, placing them, too, in some strange middle position without proper categories – the audience becomes a "non-thing". It progresses from monstrous landscape, to monster, to character, to audience.

Let's take, for example, the image of the smiling dog. Our monstrous landscape of the online environment has already been established by the nature of email forwardables, some of which are filled with viruses or scams. We already have trepidations upon opening one, or looking at the subject matter, trying to determine the truth in the experience before exploring the possibilities of opening what could be a monstrous experience. The monster of the smiling dog finds residence in this anxiety. It plants itself in this environment, drawing on the anxiety inherent in the fear of opening the wrong forwardable.

And then this is all transferred to those who look upon the image. These individuals are so deeply affected by the monster's power in the image it transforms their life. Mary E was so shaken she refused to be seen, and our narrator had to talk with her through a door. She is considered insane by the narrator, who comments how he thinks she is "off her meds". This is a common trope we have seen throughout this book so far: those who have encountered the Supernatural Other are deemed insane by those who have not. Our narrator's interactions with her are immensely notable here. They are all done through a door – never seeing her.

Here, we have a Mary E who, while alive, is not really alive in the same sense our narrator is. We cannot look at her – she's not something we can see or touch in the way we certify a reality to a presence. In many ways, she is socially dead – a way of being both alive and dead simultaneously. Jedusable in Ben Drowned is the same – he begins to withdraw from the social world he typically would place himself in, being drawn farther away from others and their constant considerations. The victims become pulled into a position that is uncomfortable and different.

The audience is involved simply through knowledge. The knowledge of the environment's monstrosity puts the audience into a position of knowledge immediately. Like the ignored and socially dead characters in the narratives, the audience's knowledge is disregarded by the others in the narrative.

It also demonstrates an understanding of fear in relation

to the understanding of the mentally ill. These authors understand that "normal" society does not treat or accept the mentally ill as one of them. They are not a part of society, but they also cannot completely reject them from society. Therefore, the social treats the mentally ill as socially dead – individuals not socially present, not worth consideration for the social category, but not so gone that they can completely disregard them. Many of the narrative we have looked at in this book reveals a consideration of the mentally ill in an attempted positive light. Even though they are painting them as socially dead, they are demonstrating how they see the outside world acting. The fear is in being considered one of them, being brought into the same consideration of socially dead and ignored. These technological monsters control the other figures in the narratives.

Those affected by these monsters are regarded as being insane and are dismissed. Jadusable in Ben Drowned described themselves as feeling their sanity slip away. The narrator of the written-out narrative of smile.jpg's narrative describes those who detail their experience as possibly being "off her meds". The characters who face the monster are faceless to the rest of society. There is much anxiety in this faceless position, where you are stripped of all your self simply due to their accidentally experience of the supernatural monster.

We have previously seen how the facelessness of characters and audience can impact the horror of the narrative of the monster. For the massive communal storytelling of creatures like the Slender Man and The Rake, much of the anxiety and the facelessness of the entire experience is in the process of telling and crafting the stories, as well as the stories themselves. The facelessness here is the relationship the characters have with the others involved. Those outside of the influence of the monsters consider those affected faceless – removed and ignored.

The facelessness is also present in the full complicated nature of the story itself. The possibilities inherent in the story means that elements may become erased purely due to other elements being clearly fictional. Others may become brought up that should be silenced simply due to the realism. The narratives themselves are full of contradictory ideas of reality and fiction, complicating the boundary between the two realms

The importance in these narratives is in the possibilities they suddenly allow. Their understanding of the monstrous landscape means they demonstrate the opportunities of the online environment, allowing some elements of monstrosity to slip through the cracks of possibilities. They allow us to see how scary the online environment itself can be – that virtual entities, whether they be video games or the internet, provide too much movement between categories. It allows for monsters to grow and flourish. We become fearful of the environment, and with that fear new monsters are able to grow and develop, allowing some to take root in our minds and grow on the possibilities these narratives provide, until the new ones grow to an even greater strength. These new narratives fully cross the boundary of reality and fiction in a way the other narratives do not.

So far, our monsters have remained fictional, even if certain elements or storytelling details cause the realism to be present. Realistic fiction, however, is still fiction. Our next chapter breaks this, bringing our digital monsters into a full realm of realism, without the fiction.

Chapter 4
Monsters That Become Real

In our previous chapter, the virtual monsters we explored revealed a level of possibility to the narratives which were not present in the previous. The massively created monsters were realistic horrific monsters, but without breaching the ultimate confines of the world of fiction. The monsters in the virtual altered this – it began to break down the boundary, even the very fine and questionable one which existed previously between the worlds of fiction and real. The virtual monsters revealed a gap in the wall, one where other monsters began to creep through, living in a strange space in which the reality of the monsters are ultimately in question.

The monsters in this chapter are often accepted as real, even if only temporarily. Often, these are built on the idea that the online environment itself is a monster, as we will see our look at Momo below. But others are brought up through the online environment as a place for the sharing of experiences you cannot share in any other environment. In either case, the digital world itself is what allows the reality of these monsters to thrive.

The Black-Eyed Kids

They almost always knock. They knock constantly and monotonously at your front door, at the window, and at your car door. There are children, aged twelve, maybe fourteen. They appeal to needing something small – just a ride somewhere, maybe a phone call – but they always want to be invited in.

And there is something strange about them. They make you feel a little dizzy, and you are on edge at the same time. The children are most often in pairs, and they always start polite. At least at first. They appeal to the speed in which the favour will take – it won't take long at all. They just want to be let in.

And their eyes are just black.

Anyone interested in the Black-Eyed Kids (BEKs) know of Brian Bethel, whose experience with BEKs is the most well-known. Bethel, a journalist, reported his experience with BEKs online in 1998. This is one of the first widely accounted for narratives on the BEKs, but believers say this is simply the most known modern BEK experience.

Bethel's experience with BEKs took place in 1996, while in Texas. He had driven to a location in the night to drop off a check for his internet provider, which was placed near a movie theatre, using the light from the theatre to write out his check. At that point, there was a knock on his driver's side window. Two young boys were outside his car, both in hoodies, between nine and twelve years old.

They appealed to Bethel that they wanted to see a movie but did not have money. They wanted a ride to their mother's house so they could pick up some money to see *Mortal Kombat*. While they continued to assure Bethel, he noticed that the last showing of *Mortal Kombat* had already started anyway. The assurances continued. It wouldn't take long.

They were just two kids. They didn't have a gun or anything. The last statement was a surprise.

When Bethel had broken the gaze with the one who was talking, suddenly the entire experience shifted. He was filled with absolute terror, and both boys had fully black eyes. He threw out whatever excuses he could think to the boys and drove away from the parking lot as soon as he could.

Bethel shared his encounter online more as a catharsis, according to him. But the narrative grew tremendously. Others began to pour out their own experiences with something similar. Some Bethel could easily discount as being just another story echoing many of the elements of his own. But others rang with a similar truth with which he found direct emotional connection. After his account went viral, Bethel withdrew as much as he could. But later, he returned to the public, more confident in his ability to share his experience.

But what are the Black-Eyed Kids? Are they some online narrative that spun out of control? Or have they existed somewhere in the world outside of the internet?

Some of these questions are simply beyond what we could try to answer here, as many paranormal investigators have taken on the exploration of the Black-Eyed Kids to a much greater depth. But we can think on definitions and characteristics of the narrative, as well as considering what role the digital environment might be able to play in the spread and proliferation of people's encounters with BEKs.

Let us start with what the BEKs even are, for those who believe or have had direct experience. This particular question is actually trickier than it might appear at first glance. Even Brian Bethel does not have a firm answer, only how it was something other, and a deep knowledge that if he had let those kids into his car back in 1996, he would not still be alive to tell the tale. Paranormal investigator David

Weatherly has a few theories. They range from the BEKs being djinn to hungry ghosts.

Interestingly, Black-Eyed Kids are sometimes interrelated with Men in Black, a phenomenon which is also sometimes associated with the Slender Man. Men in Black, unlike the Will Smith movie, are strange beings, often too thin and strangely proportioned, who visit those who have seen aliens or UFOs, or even those abducted. The Men in Black arrive, terrifyingly strange, and encourage individuals not to share their narrative, or not to pursue more investigation into the matter.

Both the BEKs and the Men in Black are sometimes described as tulpas, just as the Slender Man's playful Tulpa Theory explained its existence through the same. A tulpa, as we discussed in Chapter 2, is a thoughtform brought to life through the power of thought and suggestion. Like the Men in Black, BEKs can appear and disappear in the blink of an eye, and are unnervingly just not right, in the kind of way that's hard to put your finger on. Men in Black often enter the houses of the people they are harassing, and the individuals later question what had happened to make them do this at all. This is also similar to Bethel's account, where he describes finding his hand near the lock on the door, as if to unlock and let them in, without realising he had been considering to let them in at all.

There are many accounts of the Black-Eyed Kids outside of the internet, often spurred by online explorations of experiences. While many of the narratives are in the United States, there are also many outside, as far as the United Kingdom, Australia, South Africa and even Iraq. In the UK, there is a proliferation of experiences of BEKs in an area known as Cannock Chase, an area outside Birmingham. The sightings are frequent enough to warrant ghost walks around the town and forests, and new sightings in 2014 even made the *Huffington Post*.

Regardless of whether or not the narrative began online, individuals have had very real experiences with Black-Eyed Kids. Taking the experiences of these individuals as true, the online environment is still an important one to consider in the proliferation of experiential narratives. Research into the online environment has demonstrated that people feel the anonymity of the internet actually allows them to express more of their "true" self, than would otherwise be possible. The blurred boundaries of the internet that allowed it to be considered a monster is also what allows users to feel comfortable enough to explore their own boundaries.

Momo

But the monstrous nature of the internet is not only a good thing. The internet is already conceived of as a place of possibility for the monstrous to roam – it sometimes is seen as a frightening location in which new terrors are born and thrive. And it is this view of the internet that has given birth to Momo.

Momo became widely known in July of 2018 but rose to particular prominence in the early months of 2019. A string-haired demon girl, Momo is said to entrance children when she suddenly appears in the middle of child-geared media. She possesses them, speaking to them to give morbid instructions, which culminates in the child's suicide.

The story started with the character Momo beginning to target teenagers on WhatsApp messages. The messages were typically challenges for the player to perform a series of tasks, and when there was refusal the player was met with threats. Messages were sometimes accompanied with gory or scary images. After there was some calming over the WhatsApp messages, fear in Momo rose again in early

2019, when there were claims that Momo was beginning to appear in the middle of YouTube videos.

There were no actual reports of children who had been influenced by the Momo Challenge, or even ones driven to suicide by it appearing in the middle of a video. Despite this, police, schools and media around the world continued to report on the Momo Challenge as something verified and firmly present. Often, the media reports relied on several separated accounts, mostly through parents. The Momo Challenge reveals a certain level of fear to those who were spreading the story, but it is not children who are spreading and revealing their fears – it is parents.

To the more technologically illiterate parents, the proliferation of the internet and the inherently natural way children seem to pick it up, is already more terrifying than anything the smiling dog can make it. It is a place full of individuals the parents can't see, where a language they don't understand is spoken with words seemingly coded. It is easy to get an impression of children slipping into some unknown location, far away from parental guidance, even when the child is sitting right next to them.

And this is even before the complicated nature of the internet is revealed even more. A small glance at some of the stories we have talked about show how the internet is a place in which there are games with sincerity. The population of online trolls seems a much bigger problem – a majority instead of the minority. And the ultimate scary thing about Momo is that it meets children where they are – it does not linger just on YouTube, but also on Snap Chat. Essentially this means there is no place on the internet that is safe. The internet is both virtually and actually unsafe, with nowhere for parents to sequester their children in a virtual haven.

In many ways, the fear of the internet is similar to the fears behind other forms of popular culture, such as rock music and the fear of hidden Satanic messages in the music. Strangely, after the hoax and panic about rock music, some actually mimicked it. Similarly, questionable videos actually have found their way into YouTube Kids, including Nazi propaganda. When it came to Momo, some tried to capitalise on the sudden peak of searches by creating their own YouTube videos. While none of these exploiting Momo searches were purposely hidden or intended to hurt children, the growth of the fear in parents and media meant it opened the door for people to take advantage.

Essentially, Momo became a tulpa but in a different way. The overly concerned parents, and the massive flows of media attention, worked to breathe life into a monster which was once just a fun hoax. The more attention and thought these individuals bring to the monster, the more likely it is to find firmer ground and truly develop. In a strange twist, the more fear parents bring to the internet, the scarier the internet can become.

The Reality of Monsters Online

There is an important necessity here to explore the primary differences between our two case studies as presented here. It is clear in all knowledge and communication about the Momo Challenge that the whole story is a complete hoax. But the Black-Eyed Kids are different – there is not anything which seems to solidify the experiences regarding BEKs. Where the media relied on multiple past accounts, stories of the Black-Eyed Kids are often first-hand accounts with personal details and differences. For ease of differentiation, while also seeing some of the similar underlying elements, we can see how they are distinct through the lens of urban legend.

Jan Brunvard, who literally wrote the book on urban legends in 1981, defined the urban legend through multiple facets, the most important being how they are often heard from a friend of a friend. They are narratives of "I heard about" rather than "I experienced". Momo is a well-fitting demonstration of an urban legend in action. Media reports and parents voicing concern were never the ones who had personally experienced Momo, they were always the second or third account. And the children who were reported to having seen it never were spoken to in order to understand whether they even thought it was real. In contrast, the Black-Eyed Kids are always told from those who have encountered. They are experienced personally by many people around the world. If the reality of BEKs are in question, it is not because of the role as urban legend, but in their role as paranormal phenomenon. But there are similarities between Momo and the BEKs have nothing to do with how one is a hoax.

What we have witnessed so far is a progression of possibility in the nature of reality for monsters. Our massively created monsters enjoyed their position of fiction without losing the air of believability and realism present. There is an ever-present wink to the stories told, a slight nudge with every altered image. The in-character communication is there to purposely communicate the "real" while living in the fictional. Notes on "finding" images or stories, are ways of demonstrating a presentation of what they have done. Asking someone else for more research was the fun way of asking for more. The realism came more in the format of the narratives, such as the digitally manipulated images, mockumentary videos, and fake newspaper articles.

The virtual monsters take another step to blur the boundaries between the real and the fictional. In these cases, the believability is increased simply due to the increase in realistic elements. Lavender Town, for instance, included such realistic elements that even though the overall story of the suicides is discounted, other elements are still accepted as true; elements such as the alteration of the music from the first release to subsequent releases. The videos on YouTube of the glitched version of Ben Drowned carry a certain realistic angle – that even if the cartridge is not haunted, there must be *something* wrong with it.

All of these elements of realism lay the ground for the narratives in this chapter. The crossings of fiction and real which begins to fray and completely break down in these monsters. While all the monsters we have looked at so far question the typically conceived dichotomy between reality and fiction, these do not just question it – they break it. How the dichotomy is broken is different between BEKs and Momo, but in both cases, it is completely destroyed.

For Momo, the breaking happens because of the online environment itself. The belief in Momo started with an understanding of the internet as a monstrous location. The internet is a place in which monsters are born, bred and spread. Its own categorical breaking of existing, but not – present but not physically – sets up the online environment as a monstrous place for monsters. Like how forests and the deep sea are unfamiliar and a place for monsters, the internet is unfamiliar and full of monsters. This understanding allows for the proliferation of belief in monsters – it makes things like Momo seem all the more real.

If we can believe a video game can create background music which can cause headaches in young people, so much so they republish the game without it, then we've already cracked open the door of possibility that the virtual worlds themselves are full of monsters, with monstrous possibilities. Momo took advantage of the door only cracked open and threw it wide open. Possibility became more than just possible – it became real. Even though no one was actually inserting the strange creature of Momo in children's videos, to give morbid instructions with the purpose of causing young suicides, others believed it so fervently that according to everywhere you looked it was real. In many ways, the term "hoax" is not really accurate to describe Momo. A hoax insinuates that something did happen, but not to the same extent or with the same sincerity as initially believed. But Momo did not really exist in the first place. It didn't actually insert itself, it never caused any suicides. The whole thing was a fiction, but a fiction so believed it became truth simply through the power of the belief.

The Slender Man was given the idea of a tulpa as a way to retain a level of fear when the origin of the fiction was clearly seen. The concept was that the narrative was initially fictional but became physically manifest through the power and intensity of the thousands to millions of individuals thinking about him. But the Tulpa Theory was never taken seriously. Like the photoshopped images and the citations of fake academic texts, the Tulpa theory was presented with a nudge and a wink. It was just as much part of the fictional fun as the rest of the narratives and images.

Momo in many ways is the only true tulpa we have discussed. There were so many thoughts, so many considerations, about Momo. So much fear and attention toward the idea were poured into the monster that it was picked up. Newspapers and magazines ran with the story, warning parents about what could potentially be haunting their children. Celebrities tweeted their concern, including Kim Kardashian West who warned that parents should "pay attention" to what their children are doing. What was ultimately lost is that parents *do* know what their children are doing, but the fear is that they do not. The fear is in the environment they do not quite understand, and the lingo they can't quite decode, the relationship of videos and fiction and interactions that seem real while also seeming equally fictional.

The Black-Eyed Kids approach the door between the real and the fictional in a very different way. Instead of breaking down the boundary wall to further complicate the notions of reality and fictional with more monster creations, those who discuss BEKs online see the breakdown of reality and fiction with more possibilities.

Prior to our breaking of boundaries, we have different considerations of what counts as reality and what counts as fiction. Often, we see the description of these categories as what they consist of. Some things belong in the realm of the real, but some things do not. Things like monsters are supposed to be fictional. When the boundaries get broken down, there are more possibilities than just the ability to bring the fictional into a greater sense of real. There is also the possibility to demonstrate your own worldview as allowing some of the fictional to be real.

In other words, those who see reality as also consisting of monsters feel more restricted to discuss this aspect in places which also withhold the distinction of real and fictional which keeps monsters from being present in the real. But the internet breaks these boundaries – it explores different categories with different elements assigned to those categories. The monstrous environment of the internet actually opens the ability to talk about aspects and experiences that were once considered taboo.

We started this book with a discussion that belief is not as solid as we typically like to think. Belief is not a yes or no answer, but something which is malleable and is constantly shifting. It is something which can be performed and played with. The narratives we have studied so far enjoy the playing with belief. They perform belief and play with the various conceptions within it, which blurs our understanding. It actively demonstrates how belief is flexible and constantly altering. It demonstrates how it alters and grows with each demonstration that fiction and real is mouldable, and the level of beliefs possible within that is mouldable as well.

The play with reality the internet allows to flourish lets writers engage with the myriad of possibilities that are on the scale of belief we discussed in the intro chapter. The purpose is not about changing their own beliefs, it is not about converting or testing levels of belief. It has always been about the performance and the act of play. But this act of play allowed for a new world to grow online in which changing beliefs could be possible, even if not acted out in stories like the Slender Man or Ben Drowned.

Whether the writers who are only playing realise it or not, they created an environment of possibilities for others who are more sincere in their engagement. People who actively experienced the supernatural in their everyday lives may not have found a place to share these experiences in which the supernatural is considered real enough to actual be believed by others. Where Momo took advantage of this breakdown to further blur reality and fiction to create a stir, Brian Bethel and others like him took advantage in order to find refuge in a place in which their personal experiences may actually be believed by others. The topic of their experiences with the paranormal in their everyday life is no longer taboo – it is possible.

The reality of their experiences is actually allowed to be communicated online. These real paranormal experiences are now able to be shared widely, and through the communication of these experiences to connect to other people. All these narratives build upon one another, each one taking advantage of the elements before to build realism and possibility. This not only sets up the ability for a false narrative like Momo to take hold and transform the thoughts of fearful parents, but it also sets up the build of realism and possibilities for real narratives to be shared, to be used to connect to one another with shared narratives and shared worldviews.

The Effect of Real Monsters

Momo and the Black-Eyed Kids have two immensely similar, yet divergent, effects. Both feed on situations established and organised in the online environment, using it to their own ends, and reflecting fears and conceptions in the social world that shares them. The reflections, however, are often to slightly different ends.

The monster of Momo acts upon present fears about the internet. It lives on the idea that the internet is monstrous. Like the deep sea and the forests of old folkloric monsters, the internet is a place of the unknown to the scared parents, and it is a place of transformation for their children who are seemingly lost in the wilderness. Momo was born through the idea that children can transform through the use and exploration of the online wilderness.

In contrast, the BEKs are only present online due to the transformations the online environment provides. Where Momo's idea of the online transformation breeds fear, the BEKs are only born through a transformation of worldview and the need to connect to others with the same. A paranormal experience can alter the way someone understands the world and sees their place within it. The typical ways we categorise our understandings of life have dramatically shifted. But the shifting and transformation of the internet allows for the altered state of understanding to exist without issue. It allows a transformation of self and others through the sharing of the narratives themselves.

Both the BEKs and Momo show their effect through a relationship with children. They each have different understandings of this relationship, but children are at the heart of both fears. BEKs demonstrate a fear *toward* children. The innocence of the younger child is what the BEKs capitalise on – they assume you will be lulled into a false sense of security purely due to age. They want you to feel protective: they wish for a ride, and they are just children, so what's the harm. They want you to be lulled into a sense of security. They give comforting phrases along those lines: we're just kids, it won't take long, it's just a quick ride. It is the innocence we give children which can be altered, it can be twisted to something other. The categories of safety and danger are blurred.

Momo, on the other hand, demonstrates a fear *for* children. Children are those who are vulnerable, and unable to navigate the scary maze of the wild internet. BEKs use the line "We're just kids" as a way to attack, but for Momo the idea of "We're just kids" is a real appeal. Both the Black-Eyed Kids and Momo draw on the innocence of children – one twists the emotion to make the monster, but the other twists it to demonstrate just how scary something can be. We know we need to fear the internet because it corrupts the most vulnerable and most in need of protection.

Because the monster of Momo is only present because the online environment is scary. It's not that Momo is a monster, it's just that Momo is a facet of the monstrous internet. The internet is not safe – it is a scary place that haunts children, stalks them and corrupts them. It must be a scary place because adults do not understand it. If adults do not understand it, then how can children? The true horror of the online environment is the hidden anxieties of the parents who easily believe in the Momo monster. The parents who readily grab hold of this narrative are the ones whose greatest anxiety is the question: what are my children really doing when they are online? It draws on the anxieties of letting go, of allowing children to thrive and live in a different environment than is maybe the most comfortable.

The transformation inherent in the online environment allows for shifts in understanding. The true shift in understanding is in what can be considered true. For some, what becomes true is the slow removal of family from the self. The corruption of those most corruptible becomes real and profound – proof is unnecessary because the reality is there. It is present, and believable, and that's all that matters. For others, the shifting of what is true allows for the worldviews of others to be suddenly allowed. It gives space for new understandings of other ways to understand self, society, and the supernatural others which exist somewhere out there. The internet gives the space for these new ideas to flourish, the digital monsters of the Black-Eyed Kids exist as a reflection of what is really out there, experienced for real by real people – but with the internet as the only space in which these experiences can be expressed.

The monsters in this chapter were the most real of what we have looked at so far. For one reason or another, they have been readily accepted by those who heard of it. One of the reasons for this is due to realistic elements in previous tales being carried forward. We have already accepted certain elements as true. If we easily hold on to how those who make digital artifacts are careless enough to allow music which causes headaches, and individuals who create scary monsters can do so with a smile and the intention for it to live on its own, then it's not too much more of a step forward to think of a monster who creeps into children's videos and convinces them to self-harm. Similarly, the narratives involving experiences with Black-Eyed Kids draws on the realism in past encounters online. However, instead of the BEKs drawing on this realism in order to create a monster that others can readily grab hold of, the BEKs draw on the environment's realism created in order to foster a communal atmosphere to share paranormal experiences.

Before we conclude this chapter, it is important to mention some of the issues I have, seemingly, overlooked. I have given sympathy and understanding to the parents and media outlets who readily believed in Momo, primarily because we can look back historically as well as anthropologically in order to understand why this might be, but this is not to give a complete pass to their actions. To completely condemn a whole community simply based on what you consider to – perhaps, maybe – be true is quite frankly problematic. The whole Momo endeavour was only possible because these parents and media outlets grabbed hold of a preconceived understanding of the online environment as a place of fear and potential hurt. The result is not just a building of support around vulnerable children, it was also an attack on virtual communities which do exist and do tell stories.

When I first began doing fieldwork with communities that tell horror stories online, I faced an initial complete rejection of inclusion. When I spent time to really sit and explain the exact nature of my research, including what analytical tools I was intending on using, the conversational floodgates suddenly opened. Within twenty-four hours, I went from having a lack of responses (which had been going on for several days) to suddenly being contacted by ten community members, with another five to ten contacting over the course of the next day or so. These individuals were hesitant because I represented grander media institutions, which had the potential to twist what they were doing into something harmful and questionable. I had the potential to turn their own words against them, to remove all the winks and nudges and games being had to point at them as if they were sincerely wishing to harm others.

The communities which gave birth to the Slender Man, Ben Drowned, The Rake, and even Lavender Town Syndrome are not intending to do any harm. In fact, they completely reject violence when it is not in a fictional world. They see a difference between what one partakes in fictionally and what one does in their normal day-to-day life. Drawing any kind of connection between these community groups to intention to harm is immensely destructive to the individuals involved. And this does not even include the damage it causes to surrounding entities. The artist who initially sculpted the beautifully creepy figure used as Momo later destroyed his work due to the outcry – the outcry against something that was not even happening.

While we can understand why these parents and media outlets felt they were able to grab hold, it does not make it right. We should be wary of what fear we are allowing to grab hold of us, and what monsters we are creating through our own anxieties.

Chapter 5

Everything is True,
Even if it Isn't

The forum website reddit claims itself to be the "front page of the internet". While it sounds almost overblown, the sheer number of people who participate on the website makes it not quite as much of an exaggeration. A study in 2018 showed that reddit received 330 million users a month, with hundreds of millions of posts being added every year. Reddit is one of the most used social media sites, rivalling (if not surpassing) Facebook and Twitter.

The website is organised into subreddits, or subforums, which are centred around a particular theme or topic. These can range from serious topics, such as world news, to entertainment forms, such as video games. They can also be joined by what kind of posts are allowed, such as pictures of cute animals or pictures of houseplants. They can range from very broad to very niche.

The subreddit No Sleep is the subreddit for horror storytelling and has amassed over thirteen million subscribers. All posts are narratives written by users and they are regulated by users. Posts become more easily seen the more they are upvoted or considered good enough to be given a positive point. If narratives are deemed as low quality, a user can downvote the post, giving it a negative point. Posts can be organised by the highest ratings, allowing users to more easily find posts the community at large finds most agreeable.

The most important rule of the subreddit is the declaration "Everything is true here, even if it isn't." The rule summarises how the posts are expected to be written in first person and communicated as if true. The point is to mimic other types of subreddits you might find in which true to experience narratives are shared, such as the ever-popular entitled parents subreddit, in which users share narratives of run-ins with parents who feel entitled to special treatment. These types of subreddits are centred around first-hand accounts of personal experience. No Sleep mimics this by presenting narratives written in first person, with comments also following the play of as-if-real. The result is an atmosphere of reality, despite all knowing and engaging with the understanding of fiction.

A way of understanding how this might work is described as in-character communication. Essentially, this means users talk as-if real. Instead of directly asking for another story from an individual because they enjoy the story, they say something such as "Keep us updated" or "Have you done any more research?" This brings realism to the communication surrounding the narrative, as well as the narrative itself – the entire subreddit becomes part of the storytelling frame.

This emphasis on realism encapsulates even the nature of the narratives themselves. In previous incarnations of online monster and horror writing, such as the Slender Man mythology, the narrative often took shape in forms of "proof", such as email transcripts, digitally manipulated photos or what appears to be government documents. Unlike these early stories, No Sleep does not tell stories in these ways, but the essence is the same. While before realism came in the form of information someone might discover while doing research, such as images or newspaper articles, No Sleep relies on its realism to come from the forum itself. Reddit is often a place in which first-hand accounts are a given, and therefore No Sleep mimics this to a fictional end. First-hand accounts are more easily written as well, allowing for a multitude of individuals to participate in the storytelling, as opposed to the select few more adept as using Photoshop.

When it comes to the role of supernatural horror and the presence of monsters, the emphasis on realism becomes a heftier question filled with complications. In what mindset can a supernatural event or creature be considered "realistic"? What I consider to be possible in the world, even possible only through divine or hellish intervention, may be massively different then what is possible in your own worldview. If this were not the case, we would not have a proliferation of various religions, and even branches within those religions. When I was teaching classes on religion, I found myself encouraging the expanding of mindsets to understand and take on the possibilities of others in my students – pushing that what is supernatural and supernaturally viable for someone else is equally as valid as their own. But the subreddit No Sleep are not my students – they are writing peers to myself, and most of them much better than I am at writing.

There is no easy answer to what is considered a viable realistic horror I can provide or pave the way to. There is no single answer or description that is realistic to all. There is no catch-all understanding I can describe here. Its more nuanced, quiet, and sometimes purely lucky of who reads at what time.

The role of the community for No Sleep is of utmost importance. In older forms of horror online, the purpose was to avoid the connection between story and author. The intent was for the narratives to live online in a liminal space between reality and fiction, fully thriving on the conception of an urban legend. Narratives were understood as rationally fictional, but its detachment from author allowed it to live in a kind of urban legend level of truth. The audience could play with the concept of its reality. The moment a narrative was created and shared, it no longer belonged to the individual, but to the community and mythology at large.

There is an element of this in No Sleep, but to a much different end. On No Sleep, individual authorial connection is held as immensely important. Many writers have voiced a longing to write full-time, and they see No Sleep as how they can do that. One person in particular told me how she had been successful in this, with a movie studio picking up one of her narratives. When I was interviewing her, she was writing the script for the movie. Where other areas of creepypasta would see a narrative thriving somewhere else with no connection to author as success, the authors on No Sleep see the narrative living elsewhere *with* their name as success. On the surface, this appears to break the earlier conception of the communal authority over the individual, and to some extent this is accurate, but the community still plays an important role in the success of a narrative. The community determines which narratives are easily seen, and which become buried. While the community does not hold authorship as a collective, they as a collective do hold the authority to allow a narrative to thrive.

This chapter takes a much more directly and obvious anthropological approach than the previous ones. There are a few reasons for this. Our previous studies have been more historical in how we look at things. Despite the actual bit of analysis being more anthropological, using anthropology to better understand what the monsters are doing for people, our look back is always more historical simply due to the nature of what we are looking at. Something like the Slender Man and The Rake happened in the past, though its effects and its retellings reverberate through time. No Sleep is a bit different because it's much more contemporary. Much of what is happening is still happening at the time of writing.

Narrative Case Studies

In April of 2018, reddit user u/athousandrows wrote a story entitled "I met someone who claimed to be the devil… and I think I believe them", which became very highly rated on the subreddit. At time of writing, it is still among the highest ratings of all time for the subreddit.[1]

The story follows a young man who goes to a pub late at night in London, after abandoning friends at a club. There, he meets a seemingly drunk young woman, with fiery red hair. She introduces herself as Lucifer, or Lucy for short. What follows is a narrative of the exchanges between Lucy and the narrator, who talk about Lucy's life and feelings toward humans. The narrative culminates in her revealing the truth of Hell, shocking the narrator to his core.

This story demonstrates the best functions of supernatural horror as they are typically found on No Sleep. Before more general comments are made, I should stress that it is difficult to make comments about the entirety of all narratives on all the subreddit due to the sheer volume of narratives, which are constantly being added to with every

---

1 The following paragraph is a quick summary of "I met someone who claimed to be the devil… and I think I believe them" by u/athousandrows, originally posted April 2018, shared here with permission from the author. I have not included all narrative points, to maintain narrative integrity to the original. Please take the time to read the original work, which can be found at https://www.reddit.com/r/nosleep/comments/8chsch/i_met_someone_who_claimed_to_be_the_devil_and_i/

minute that passes. To give an idea of the numbers involved, the subreddit No Sleep hosts fourteen million subscribers, which doesn't account for anyone who goes onto the subreddit manually, or who partakes in No Sleep narratives through other forms, such as podcasts or YouTube videos. Even if only half those participants are active writers on the subreddit, that would still account for seven million writers posting new narratives every single day. It is, quite frankly, unfeasible to attempt to say something about everything present on all the narratives.

That being said, there are certain generalisations which could be made, and most of them in relation to how the subreddit approaches the question of the realistic supernatural other. Most of the narratives which do involve supernatural elements include it in two primary ways: the first is in an echo of Judeo-Christian theology, and the second is in a more questionable cosmic horror which echoes Lovecraft.

Our case study here demonstrates this first version of realistic supernatural elements. The narrative centres around the figure of the Christian devil, even though the presentation of the devil is slightly different than what is typically considered. In contrast, other presentations of the supernatural are less obvious about its topic. These are often more questionable – the horror in the answers left unsaid.

An example of the more questioning type can be found in the story by u/EaPAtbp, "My sugar daddy asks me for weird favors".[2] In this narrative, the narrator receives texts from a new sugar daddy, but one who does not want sexual favours, but rather asks for small strange errands to be carried out. Instructions are strange and specific, and the reality of what is occurring is left without direct explanation.

---

2 As previously, this is the briefest of references to be made to this narrative. For a full reading, please read u/EaPAtbp's work "My sugar daddy asks me for weird favors" found at https://www.reddit.com/r/nosleep/comments/diuucz/my_sugar_daddy_asks_me_for_weird_favors/

A lot of the more questioning type of approach is similar to the work of H.P Lovecraft. Lovecraft's vision of our world is marred with the presence of the Ancient Ones: old, almost supernatural entities which are not of this world. They are constructed of non-Euclidian geometry and their names and words are not meant to be spoken by any conception of language from our world. They are wholly Other.

Lovecraft's approach to horror is what he calls "cosmic horror": an instinctual feeling of such awe and fear that it captures the feeling of a religious experience. Often cited simultaneously with Lovecraft is Rudolf Otto, an early scholar of religion who described the feeling of the religious as being mysterious, tremendous and fascinating, a strangely terrifying, awe-inspiring, and wholly incomprehensible experience. Lovecraft's idea of cosmic fear is exactly this, a conception and experience which cannot be fully explained or even fully understood by the human mind. Lovecraft wrote:

> The one test of the really weird is simply this – whether or not there be excited in the reader a profound sense of dread, and of contact with unknown spheres and powers; a subtle attitude of awed listening, as if for the beating of black wings or the scratching of outside shapes and entities on the known universe's utmost rim.

The questioning recalls cosmic horror. When we appeal to the more traditional Judeo-Christian settings of what supernaturally is present, then we do not have to leave the question open-ended: its available and known. Its scarier to know who the devil is, to identify Lucy as her, than to leave the reader as simply open-ended. Many writers on No Sleep have just as many struggles with the relationship between the supernatural and the real as I did when first looking at No Sleep and considering the conception of a realistic supernatural monster – my time as anthropologist with No Sleep revealed a lot of intricate details involving the negotiation of real and supernatural monster.

Living on the Forums

Contemporary anthropological approaches to research are based on one primary understanding: a researcher can gain the greatest understanding of a community by directly interacting with the community as much as possible. It may seem common sense, but this was done in reaction to many earlier scholars who found it unnecessary to travel and talk to others in order to truly study them. Bronislaw Malinowski was one of the first to demonstrate how an anthropologist can conduct their studies.

At the heart of anthropological research is a mimicking of a small child who asks too many questions. Why do you wear the clothes you wear when you wear them? Why do you talk to one person differently than another? We must talk to those in the communities we study with open minds and questions of proper exploration, pushing for thoughts that, admittedly, the community may not have even asked in the first place. And the scholar must also live with the community. For some, this means travelling to remote villages, armed with nothing but a journal, a digital voice recorder and a machete. For me, I travelled into the depths of the subreddit No Sleep, armed with curiosity and a somewhat lacking ability to write fiction.

Anthropologists call the engagement with the community participant-observation because that's essentially what it is. We not only observe what is occurring, but we try to *participate* as much as possible. During my time "living" on the subreddit No Sleep, I drafted my own horror stories to be involved in the process. I hoped the practice would teach me about the methods of communication about the narrative. My actual experience taught me how nerve-wracking it is to write and submit the narrative for the subreddit's approval, or most-often disapproval, as well as how complicated the idea of realistic horror is.

I ended up having to write two stories. My first was deleted by the subreddit for not being horror enough. The deletion of my writing was definitely a blow to the ego. I like to think of myself as a decent writer. I felt I had drafted something which blurred what could possibly be happening, attempting to not take any stance on any side of realistic horror. It obviously did not work. My second narrative took a much more direct approach, although still leaving the full questions of what exactly the monster was left unanswered. The role of the supernatural was still heavily present, and heavily obvious.

The process made me rethink the idea of a realistic supernatural from the point of view of the writer, rather than as the reader I had been until then, and especially from the perspective of a writer who had previously failed. The ratings caused me indescribable levels of anxiety – I found myself checking the rating every few hours after posting. The story remained part of me, as the individual author –as opposed to the writing of a Slender Man narrative for instance – but it also suddenly belonged to the community to judge.

The complicated nature of the "real" in supernatural horror rests in the understanding of how the narrative bridges a gap between reality and fiction. My narrative must, in some way, be obviously fictional, while also being realistic enough to cause a horrified reaction in the minds of the audience. Most important is the role of the question "what if?".

When talking to writers during my fieldwork, they seemed to immediately renounce the idea of including a supernatural element in the writing, but most backtracked quite quickly in the conversation by amending it to comment how it must be "realistic", although what made one supernatural narrative more realistic than another was not as obvious directly. However, through a deeper understanding of all aspects of our conversations, we can start to understand a little better.

Many participants voiced the importance of true crime narratives as inspiration, most notably those which are quietly mysterious and leaves the lingering question of "what if?" in the minds of the listeners. One conversation I had was with a user who felt particularly compelled by the story of Elisa Lam.

Elisa Lam was a twenty-one-year-old Canadian university student, found dead at the Cecil Hotel in Los Angeles on January 31, 2013. Her body was found floating in one of the hotel's water tanks and many other details have remained mysterious. Adding to the mystery, as well as inspiring the internet to help, was a released surveillance video of Lam in the elevator of the hotel. The video, released by the police to find her when still missing, depicted Lam acting very oddly. She steps into the elevator and pushes all the floor buttons. She keeps stepping in and out of the elevator door, always looking toward the hallways of the hotel. The end of the video shows Lam standing by the door, moving her hands in strange gestures. No one else was captured on the video. The question of how Lam ended up in the water tank, and what the surveillance video truly meant, led to much speculation. The video of her elevator experience reached tens of millions of views and set the internet on a race to find the best theory to explain what happened.

What is interesting about the particular conversation I had

with my No Sleep writer regarding Elisa Lam was the emphasis put on the more mysterious occurrences surrounding her death. Despite the true nature of the crime, the video footage of the elevator can easily lead an individual to the possibility something other than natural was occurring. It was excitedly commented to me that perhaps she could see something we could not. Not in the same sense of a mental break, which is sometimes concluded for Lam, but rather we are incapable of seeing something she was capable of. The more supernatural consideration of the events surrounding her death gives her more agency, but also leverages a sense of possibility, and potentially realism, to supernatural occurrences surrounding an unfortunate death.

Michael Kinsella, a researcher at University of California, Santa Barbara, wrote about legend-trippers, or when people travel to a specific location or perform specific actions which, according to a legend, has the potential to trigger a supernatural experience. He described how legend-trippers perform the strange intermingling between fantasy and reality, with the purpose more toward the engaging with the emotion behind a performance, rather than in proving the supernatural as real. Writers like my excited participant are a flipped nature of Kinsella's legend-trippers. Kinsella writes how legend-trippers combine the nature of folklore with forms of fiction, most notably Lovecraft's Cthulhu Mythos. Several versions of the once fictional Necronomicon have now been fully published by those interested in the occult. These writers claim Lovecraft had unknowingly tapped into an occult reality but had ascribed it to his imagination instead. The writers on No Sleep flip this; instead of bringing the fictional into the real, they bring the real into the fictional through the exploration of true crime narratives and the emphasis on the realistic nature of both narrative and communication about narratives.

What is interesting about the nature of the ultimate question of "what if?" is the open acceptance of some aspects of supernatural monstrosity over others. The devil's existence is much more of a given then, say, a ghost. Even if a writer, or an audience member, is not in the waters of belief regarding Christian ideas of the devil or Hell, they are still standing around it due to the nature of the worldviews they grew up around. No Sleep is an English-speaking subreddit, and therefore is typically dominated by residences of primarily English-speaking countries, most of which are dominated culturally speaking by Christianity. But that does not mean the realm of ghosts, or even other supernatural elements are not impossible – they just need to be engaged with "realistically". This means hints at what might be possible, pulling into the avenue of possibility.

The narratives themselves use the blurring of fiction and reality in order to push the possibilities of what's real, sometimes relying on cosmic fear in order to push the possible reality a little further. Unlike other forms of fiction which attempt to be as realistic as possible to draw readers into the world, writers of online horror such as those on No Sleep, are not writing realistically in order to convince or suspend disbelief, rather writers use realism in order to play the game of as if reality.

The play with reality, even in terms of the supernatural, allow writers to engage with the myriad of possibilities which exist within every scale of belief. The purpose, however, is not about changing their own beliefs. They are not engaging with the supernatural in order to decide whether to convert. Rather, it is more about the performance itself.

Back to the Fiction

This book, so far, has taken us through a variety of explorations of how fiction and reality interplay with one another. In our introduction, we saw how early horror played with the boundaries between fiction and reality through the use of epistemological framing. Mary Shelley's *Frankenstein* played with the boundaries between fiction and reality while still living in the firm place of fiction. It used realistic narrative tools, while also drawing on the foundations of differing levels of belief and possibility. She added bits of cosmic fear where necessary to allow a dangling of reality in the fiction, to draw ideas in and deeply engage with the "what if?".

The massively created monsters, like the Slender Man and The Rake, were created realistically in order to fool, and to give winks and nods to possibilities while still living fully in the realm of fiction. Those who read and wrote Slender Man narratives never fully believed in the reality of the story. We then took another step into some of the narratives which focused on the realm of the virtual itself. Here, the online environment made some believe a bit more in the realism of the narrative. It made realistic elements stand out a bit more, even when they were crafted. While the full narrative still remained in the fiction, some elements were carried forward due to the perceived reality, being more convincing due to the nature of the monstrous environment. We then saw how these nuggets of truth can lay the foundation for bringing real narratives and real monsters to life.

This chapter brought things back to what we saw at the very beginning. The writers on No Sleep are the contemporary Gothic writers, who use the new forms of journal writing and letters to build the framing of realism. All of this is done without losing the firm foundation of fiction.

Much of the difference between the massive communally created monsters and No Sleep is in the grounding of fiction and the relationship of the author to the text. The point of crafting the realistic narratives for the massively created monsters is to have the narrative live completely separate from the author. Success is in seeing your narrative replicated in a variety of ways in other places, with no tie to what you contributed, or even if you contributed. Because of this intention, the foundation which screams fiction is more cracked – not gone, just cracked. In contrast, No Sleep is a place of authorship, where the narrative is tied to author, and remains tied to author. Finding the story somewhere else separate from author is a transgression, and therefore the foundation of fiction remains intact. Our writers on No Sleep are the new Mary Shelleys.

That is not to say there is still no play happening here. The play is just as present as it was for our Gothic writers – a play of "as if". The boundary between reality and fiction cracks in a playful way. Writers and audiences have fun with the narratives and the realism possible, without needing to have some ultimate purpose behind it beyond crafting a good story.

Anthropologist Claude Lévi-Strauss is a foundational figure in the study of myth. He explored the notion of mythic thought as always working from a knowledge of oppositions, to their eventual reconciliation. Whether it is consciously or unconsciously done, the writers on No Sleep are engaging with an inherent binary: the real and the fictional. The as if play in their stories begin to bridge the gap, resulting in some kind of mediation in the previously separated worlds. The play with belief brings the whole experiences to a middle ground.

The process of play, therefore, creates mythic thinking, and mythic thinking can create spiritual experiences. These experiences are not necessarily as overt as those created by Kinsella's legend-trippers but they undoubtedly allow for the writer's mind to actively engage with conceptions of the supernatural which fit within their preconceived notion of possible reality. My participant who spoke specifically of Elisa Lam, for instance, told her story with a type of intensity which made me feel he was living vicariously through it, seeing a supernatural experience of horror ready to be told. The process of writing allows them to shift from somewhere off a scale of belief to on it – able to immerse themselves while never losing the constant fictional lens.

The importance is on the performance and formatting of the narrative itself. It is not about changing belief when they play. It's about a manipulation of belief – it's a direct engagement with the fuzziness of the word, to shift it and mould it for their own purpose.

When I first began to chat with writers, I asked if they enjoyed writing or reading horror which involved supernatural monsters. Most immediately rejected the idea but began to recount when they said the supernatural was acceptable and scary when it was what they deemed as "realistic". The idea of what is even considered "supernatural" to begin with is often based on preconceived ideas of how the world works: what is supernatural is simply what is outside of what is natural. If the actions of gods or spirits are simply part of the understanding of the world, it is not exactly *super*natural, now is it? Writers can employ aspects of the supernatural that, at one point, were deemed as too otherworldly to be considered real – sometimes utilising aspects of cosmic fear to bring conceptions of this to be more realistic. The process of making these aspects more real to them actually allows the writers to negotiate once differing worldviews.

A shifting of an understanding of the world is already a process some of the writers have gone through. One participant responded to a question about why they write horror with a lengthy explanation of past childhood trauma, and how the writing of horror helped to cope with their new reality. Traumatic events may change the way an individual sees the world, shifting the original conception of reality to one which can incorporate their experience.

In many ways, the writers on No Sleep are like those who share their experiences of the Black-Eyed Kids. For believers in BEKs, the experience with the supernatural shifted their previous understanding of the world, demonstrating a new worldview. The conversation about them, including the negotiation of what they may be, is an attempt to make the new shifting of understanding to make sense. The writers on No Sleep, on the other hand, are doing so to a more fictional end. They negotiate the boundaries of their own reality to demonstrate the alterations of reality often felt by themselves, or even the characters within their narratives. Horror writing is a way for them to describe their experiences with an agency normally not provided to them. It allows them to depict the transitioning of these worldviews and the negotiation of new ways to consider the world around them.

The play with belief depicts the process of bringing the supernatural into the everyday, as well as bringing the everyday into the supernatural. The entire process, the negotiation of boundaries between reality and fiction and how this involves the role of the supernatural, is what makes the entirety of the world possible. And through this, everything is true, even if it isn't.

Final Thoughts
The Future of Digital Monsters

My face is only lit by the soft blue glow of my computer screen, and I keep promising that soon, just after this story, I'll finally go to sleep. The encroaching darkness makes me cuddle further into my computer, curled around hot tea as my only comfort. The radiators click. I jump at every small noise. The monsters I read on the screen are all around me, looming ever closer with each story. And I know that monsters are real.

Throughout this book, we have seen there are four levels of how reality and fiction can cross and break the boundaries between themselves. The subreddit No Sleep, what is arguably now the largest centre for online horror storytelling, recalls the older ways of storytelling. The writers on No Sleep echo the older English Gothic writers, who once relied on framing the novels in journals and diary entries to impart a level of realism to the narratives. No Sleep relies on the formatting of the subreddit, and the expectations of the website in order to impart realism to their narratives. The interactions and the emphasis that "everything is true, even if it isn't" allows a fun game of as-if in which individuals play with the realistic conceptions of supernatural monsters without losing the grounding of fiction.

Communally constructed monsters, such as the Slender

Man and The Rake, take this grounding of realism one step further. The massive nature of many individuals all contributing to the same narrative at the same time means the authorial control given to Gothic narratives and No Sleep is gone. Complete control is given to the community. And with this, a level of realism is almost necessary. In-character communication allows flow of narrative between individuals without sacrificing the game of "as if". The formatting of the narrative also shifts: instead of first-person accounts, there are digitally manipulated images and videos, faked newspapers and citations from non-existent academic texts. The communally constructed monsters cracked the foundation of fiction that the Gothic and No Sleep maintain. These still have not lost their grounding in fiction, but there are fractures with in.

The virtual monsters we looked at further cracked this foundation, giving small glimpses of possible realities very easily believed, even if the monsters themselves are not. The Lavender Town Syndrome, while not fully believed, was given just enough realistic elements that these small aspects to the story were easily grabbed hold of, even if the grander narrative was discounted. These more realistic elements further cracked foundations, breaking the boundaries between reality and fiction by allowing fictional elements to be firmly believed and therefore brought into reality.

The virtual monsters allowed for the monsters which do cross into reality to thrive. The virtual let people begin to believe in the monstrous location of the internet – that this was a place where bad things grew and developed. The online environment became the place where monsters live, the only place where modern people in the English-speaking world believe monsters dwell. This allowed the Momo conspiracy theory to thrive. Of course a monster like Momo would exist, one who prowls the internet to find vulnerable children. They pray on children like the old fairies prowling forests preys on children. But this alteration of the landscape also allows people with genuine experiences of paranormal monsters to share their experiences and connect to others who feel the same.

There are cyclical ways in which these explorations occur, and one feeds into the other. The implications of the monster becoming real, and the violent reactions against the environment and these storytelling mechanisms by those outside looking in, often causes people to turn back. They revert to other, more real, forms in reaction. But that is not to say all of these are not happening simultaneously at various points in time. The Momo conspiracy, for instance, was occurring at the same time as No Sleep's popularity.

Interestingly, the communally created narratives are not quite as popular right now. The height of popularity for these created narratives was between the late 2000s and the early 2010s. The Slender Man is arguably the most prominent of this type of narrative. He spread along the internet quickly and with a power only mythology and storytelling can really do. However, after the Wisconsin Stabbings in 2014, the landscape completely altered. Forum sites dedicated to the Slender Man began to shut down, and the community was never really able to recover. Regardless of how the community rejects real world violence, and sees such an act as unrepresentative of them, the outside media forces did not see it this way and flung blame on the community. The consequence was a disruption of a functioning community and its resultant annihilation.

Monsters constructed similarly to the Slender Man have not really existed in quite the same way. Other narratives have grown like the Slender Man, such as the Twitch Plays Pokémon mythology, but monsters have not really taken root in quite the same way. And the media fervour against the online community's construction of a monster allows the shifting to possible realities to be more prevalent. The internet is a place where monsters are born, whether they really are or not.

The current state of online monsters is primarily based around No Sleep. Even though the narratives are centred on realism, there is still a strong foundation of fiction to the narratives. This foundation is the safest way for the communities who enjoy telling stories to do so while not arousing the anger of those who do not quite understand other forms of monster creation and telling

Occasionally, monsters still appear, appearing in the crossover between reality and fiction. Momo crossed over most recently, rising to the greatest prominence in 2018 and 2019. The reality of Momo was only possible due to the great fear the online environment itself generates to those who are less technologically literate and knowledgeable, and for those who see the faceless storytelling participants as possible of creating great monsters.

The vast majority of people in the outside world can easily believe in the monstrosity of the online environment due to the easily grabbed elements of realism in some of the previous narratives, as well as in the great technological growth. The grabbing at this reality, even for those less prevalent in digital communities, actually allows the growth of digital monsters. Momo did not actually happen, but the heavy level of belief given to it allowed the monster to become real and possible in the minds of those who believed in the monstrosity of the online environment.

Monsters, whether they are digital or not, are always on some level real. Even those who are deemed as only living in books and movies carry a reality with them. Monsters are real in the *effect* they have on the society and community which tells them. Vampires demonstrate the anxieties present in what exists between the dichotomies of life and death, werewolves the possibilities of a joining of human and animal. Some of the anxieties digital monsters represent were explored as we went through the text: the anxiety of the middle ground position of physical and virtual that virtual communities reveal; or the anxiety in parents who feel disconnected from their children, and fear they don't know what is happening with them.

Digital monsters demonstrate the greatest anxiety is about the online environment itself. The internet gives us a monstrous place – the virtual wilderness which allows transformation of self, society and monster. Where monsters once prowled forests and the deepest seas, they now prowl the digital worlds, existing in the space between screens.

The online environment is a new format through which communication and storytelling occurs. But at its heart, the communication and storytelling which occurs in these environments are not anything new or different to what's been going on for ages. Storytelling is fundamentally performance based, and even when developed virtually it is performance focused. No matter how the relationship between participants and the virtual environment may develop and change, the interaction and communication between peoples more generally will not disappear. Despite this communication occurring via computer screens and the internet, it still involves humans, acting and interacting in a very human venture. Storytelling is fundamentally human: we are simply narratives wrapped in flesh. The internet and the rise of the virtual has not dehumanised interaction, it has simply altered the means through which this communication occurs.

Storytelling is always a communication of cultural and social ideas. They are made up of cultural memories and social knowledge; we manage and transmit these ideas, memories and knowledge through the process of storytelling. Monsters are no different – in fact, they are the transmission of social and cultural fears and anxieties. As time and society progresses, so do the technologies we use. But it is important to keep in mind that every username has a human on the other side, still thinking, acting, and performing stories like humans do.

Any new monster waiting to be born will most likely be easily believed. It will grab hold of the same environment Momo did, holding onto the anxieties already present regarding the online environment. The monstrosity of the environment is already easily believed – it carries with it the social and cultural memories of past perceived transgressions. It also carries previous anxieties regarding popular cultural more generally speaking, such as rock and roll music. Therefore, future monsters will capitalise on these foundational fears. The monster will be scary because it carries with it the anxieties of years before. This, paired with the belief in the monstrosity of the online environment itself, will allow for the monster to be created. It could be created by the belief in the monster's existence, as was beginning to be hinted at with Momo.

But there is another possibility, though not necessarily one which is mutually exclusive from the creation of a real monstrous hoax. It is possible the current situation of No Sleep's firm fictionality will last a little longer. Over time, there will be a shifting back to what we saw in the cycle of monstrous creation: communally created narratives will rise once again.

If anything is possible in the world of humanity, it is humans' incessant ability to repeat everything they have done before, whether intentionally or not. Just because the communally created narratives have died down in prominence does not mean they will not find a foothold again.

At some point, the community will want to band together anew, telling stories together the way they used to.

Tulpas have formed a large portion of the conversations around digital monsters. For some, tulpas became the primary form through which their existence was explained. The Slender Man leant on the presence of tulpas in order to explain how a monster can be fiction and reality at the same time. Momo, on the other hand, was a tulpa in a truer sense. The more the greater outside media and scared parents believed in the reality of Momo, the more it opened the door for the possibility for something like Momo to really exist. Not only that, but the fact that Momo didn't actually exist, nor was doing the acts which were prescribed to her, didn't matter; it still existed in the minds and responses to everyone around. Momo became a tulpa through the force of the thoughts of those involved.

Like a tulpa, digital monsters create a life for themselves outside of the narratives alone, building on those who know of them and think about them. In many ways, this book itself is also a contribution to this, getting all readers to continue to think about the monsters and grow, an encouragement to think and understand monsters is also an encouragement to understand monsters as inherently real in their effect. And their effect is more than just the exploration of anxieties present in the communities which create and share them; they also give the communities a level of agency and individual creativity which deserves to be celebrated. They provide ways for individuals to play with their own cultural understandings and thoughts, whatever level of reality they are given.

The idea of any of these monsters going "viral" is to miss the most important part of what they are doing. The idea of "viral" is a metaphor for a medical virus, one which takes over people without any consent from the body involved.

It makes users on the internet seem passive in their consumption, while, in reality, they are much more involved in the process. Consumers, even online, are not passive in the engagement of what is around them – they have a direct agency over what is successful and what is not.

These monsters are not viral, but an active part of the community. It is the agency given to individual creators and to the community more largely speaking which allows their images, stories and narratives to spread online like the haunted figures they are. And their presence allows others the courage and space to share narratives of other figures, whose reality is more in question, like those with experiences of the Black-Eyed Kids.

So, when reading narratives online, sat on my bed with the only lighting of the screen, I jump at the small noises in my house. I jump because the monsters are real, stalking the darkness around me, shouting back at me the anxieties, questions, memories and realities of the social worlds who originally spun them. I read them to life, speak them to life, and share them to life.

Because monsters are real. You just have to look for them.

References

Chapter 1: Introducing the Monsters of the Digital Worlds

Asma, Stephen T. 2009. *On Monsters: An Unnatural History of Our Worst Fears*. New York: Oxford University Press.

Beattie, James. 1809. 'On Fable and Romance'. In *The Works of James Beattie: Dissertations, Moral and Critical*. Vol. 3. The Works of James Beattie. Hopkins and Earle.

Blank, Trevor J. 2009. 'Introduction: Toward a Conceptual Framework for the Study of Folklore and the Internet'. In *Folklore and the Internet: Vernacular Expression in a Digital World*, 1–20. Logon, Utah: Utah University Press.

Carroll, Noël. 1990. *The Philosophy of Horror, or, Paradoxes of the Heart*. New York: Routledge.

Chase. 2014. 'TPP Victory! The Thundershock Heard Around the World'. *Twitch. Tv* (blog). 1 March 2014. https://blog.twitch.tv/tpp-victory-the-thundershock-heard-around-the-world-3128a5b1cdf5.

Cohen, Jeffrey J. 1996. 'Monster Culture (Seven Theses)'. In *Monster Theory: Reading Culture*, edited by Jeffrey J. Cohen, 1–20. Minneapolis, MN: University of Minnesota Press.

Dawkins, Richard. 2006. *The Selfish Gene*. 30th anniversary ed. Oxford ; New York: Oxford University Press.

Day, Abby. 2011. *Believing in Belonging: Belief and Social Identity in the Modern World*. Oxford: Oxford University Press.

Douglas, Mary. 1966. *Purity and Danger: An Analysis of the Concepts of Pollution and Taboo*. London: Routledge.

Gilmore, David D. 2003. *Monsters: Evil Beings, Mythical Beasts, and All Manner of Imaginary Terrors*. Philadelphia: University of Pennsylvania Press.

Hernandez, Patricia. 2014. 'Rejoice, for "Twitch Plays Pokemon" Has Revived the Helix Fossil'. *Kotaku* (blog). 24 February 2014. https://kotaku.com/rejoice-for-twitch-plays-pokemon-has-revived-the-hel-1529832673.

Lovecraft, H.P. 1973. *Supernatural Horror in Literature*. New York: Dover Publications.

Mittman, Asa Simon. 2013. 'Introduction: The Impact of Monsters and Monster Studies'. In *The Ashgate Research Companion to Monsters and the Monstrous*, edited by Asa Simon Mittman and Peter Dendle, 1–16. Ashgate Research Companions. Farnham, Surrey: Ashgate.

Musharbash, Yasmine, and Geir Henning Presterudstuen, eds. 2014. *Monster Anthropology in Australasia and Beyond*. First edition. New York, NY: Palgrave Macmillan.

Shifman, Limor. 2014. *Memes in Digital Culture*. MIT Press Essential Knowledge. Cambridge, Massachusetts: The MIT Press.

Tompkins, J.M.S. 1962. *The Popular Novel in England, 1770-1800*. London: Methuen.

Chapter 2: Massively Created Monsters

Asimos, Vivian. forthcoming. *Digital Mythology and the Internet's Monster*. Bloomsbury Academic, An imprint of Bloomsbury Publishing Plc.

Besant, Annie, and C.W Leadbetter. 1925. *Thought-Forms*. London: Theosophical Publishing House Ltd.

Blue Isle Studios, and Parsec Productions. 2015. *Slender: The Arrival*. Xbox One.

Bohn, Willard. 1991. *Apollinaire and the Faceless Man: The Creation and Evolution of a Modern Motif*. Rutherford, N.J. : London ; Cranbury, NJ: Fairleigh Dickinson University Press ; Associated University Presses.

Chess, Shira, and Eric Newsom. 2015. *Folklore, Horror Stories, and Slender Man: The Development of an Internet Mythology*. Palgrave Pivot. New York: Palgrave Pivot.

David-Néel, Alexandra. 1936. *With Mystics and Magicians in Tibet*. London: Penguin.

Evans-Wentz, Walter Y., ed. 1960. *The Tibetan Book of the Dead or: The after-Death Experiences on the Bardo Plane, According to Lama Kazi Dawa-Samdups English Rendering*. 2. publ. Delhi: Oxford University Press.

Gerogerigege. 2009. 'Create Paranormal Images'. Forum Post. *Something Awful*. https://forums.somethingawful.com/showthread.php?threadid=3150591&userid=0&perpage=40&pagenumber=1.

Lovecraft, H.P. 1973. *Supernatural Horror in Literature*. New York: Dover Publications.

Mikles, N. L., and J. P. Laycock. 2015. 'Tracking the Tulpa: Exploring the "Tibetan" Origins of a Contemporary Paranormal Idea'. *Nova Religio: The Journal* of Alternative and Emergent Religions 19 (1): 87–97. https://doi.org/10.1525/nr.2015.19.1.87.

Parsec Productions. 2012. *Slender: The Eight Pages*. PC.

Peck, Andrew. 2015. 'Tall, Dark, and Loathsome: The Emergence of a Legend Cycle in the Digital Age'. *Journal of American Folklore* 128 (509): 333–48.

Plattor, Candace. 2014. '12-Year-Olds Stabbing 12-Year-Olds: Are We Paying Attention Yet?' Canadace Plattor. 4 June 2014. http://candaceplattor.com/blog/12-year-olds-stabbing-12-year-olds-are-we-paying-attention-yet/.

rinski. 2009. 'Create Paranormal Images'. Forum Reply. *Something Awful*. https://forums.somethingawful.com/showthread.php?threadid=3150591&userid=0&perpage=40&pagenumber=39.

Slender Nation Podcast. 2011. *VICTOR @#$%ING SURGE*. Podcast Episode.

Victor Surge. 2009a. 'Create Paranormal Images'. Forum Reply. *Something Awful*. https://forums.somethingawful.com/showthread.php?threadid=3150591&userid=0&perpage=40&pagenumber=3.

———. 2009b. 'Create Paranormal Images'. Forum Reply. *Something Awful*. https://forums.somethingawful.com/showthread.php?threadid=3150591&userid=0&perpage=40&pagenumber=4.

Chapter 3: Virtual Monsters and Monstrous Video Games

Alex Hall. 2010a. *Day Four.Wmv*. YouTube Video.

———. 2010b. *BEN.Wmv*. YouTube Video.

———. 2010c. *DROWNED.Wmv*. YouTube Video.

———. 2010d. *Jadusable.Wmv*. YouTube Video.

———. 2010e. *Free.Wmv*. YouTube Video.

Asimos, Vivian. forthcoming. *Digital Mythology and the Internet's Monster*. Bloomsbury Academic, An imprint of Bloomsbury Publishing Plc.

Brunvand, Jan Harold. 1981. *The Vanishing Hitchhiker: American Urban Legends and Their Meanings*. 1st ed. New York: Norton.

Carroll, Noël. 1990. *The Philosophy of Horror, or, Paradoxes of the Heart*. New York: Routledge.

Creepypasta Indexer. 2013. 'The Curious Case of Smile.Jpg'. Creepypasta.Org. 10 April 2013. http://www.creepypasta.org/creepypasta/the-curious-case-of-smile-jpg.

Douglas, Mary. 1966. *Purity and Danger: An Analysis of the Concepts of Pollution and Taboo*. London: Routledge.

Kibby, Marjorie D. 2005. 'Email Forwardables: Folklore in the Age of the Internet'. *New Media & Society* 7 (6): 770–90. https://doi.org/10.1177/1461444805058161.

Leach, Edmund. 1972. 'Anthropological Aspects of Language: Animal Categories and Verbal Abuse'. In *Mythology; Selected Readings*, edited by Pierre Maranda, 39–67. Penguin Modern Sociology Readings. Harmondsworth, Eng., Baltimore: Penguin Books.

Lévi-Strauss, Claude. 1963. 'The Structural Study of Myth'. In *Structural Anthropology*, translated by C. Jacobson and B.G. Schoepf, 206–31. New York: Basic Books.

———. 1969. *The Raw and the Cooked*. Translated by John Weightman and Doreen Weightman. Introduction to a Science of Mythology / Claude Lévi-Strauss, v. 1. Chicago: University of Chicago Press.

Zipes, Jack. 1988. *The Brothers Grimm: From Enchanted Forests to the Modern World*. New York: Routledge.

Chapter 4: Monsters That Become Real

Bargh, John A, A McKenna, and Grainne M. Fitzsimons. 2002. 'Can You See the Real Me? Activation and Expression of the "true Self" on the Internet'. *Journal of Social Issues* 58 (1): 33–48.

Bethel, Brian. 2013. 'Brian Bethel Recounts His Possible Paranormal Encounter with "BEKs"'. *Abilene Reporter-News*, 13 April 2013. https://web.archive.org/web/20151208221117/http://www.reporternews.com/news/columnists/brian-bethel/brian-bethel-recounts-his-possible-paranormal-encounter-with-beks-ep-384772497-348207271.html.

Brunvand, Jan Harold. 1981. *The Vanishing Hitchhiker: American Urban Legends and Their Meanings*. 1st ed. New York: Norton.

Day, Abby. 2011. *Believing in Belonging: Belief and Social Identity in the Modern World*. Oxford: Oxford University Press.

Kissel, Ben, Marcus Parks, and Henry Zebrowski. n.d. 'Ep. 323: Men in Black Part I: You Fed the Tulpa'. Last Podcast on the Left. Accessed 30 June 2018. https://soundcloud.com/lastpodcastontheleft/episode-323-the-men-in-black.

Redfern, Nicholas. 2011. *The Real Men in Black: Evidence, Famous Cases, and True Stories of These Mysterious Men and Their Connection to UFO Phenomena*. Pompton Plains, NJ: New Page Books.

Robertson, David G. 2016. *UFOs, Conspiracy Theories and the New Age: Millennial Conspiracism*. Bloomsbury Advances in Religious Studies. London ; New York: Bloomsbury Academic, An imprint of Bloomsbury Publishing Plc.

Weatherly, David. 2017. *The Black Eyed Children*.

Chapter 5: Everything is True, Even if it Isn't

athousandrows. 2018. 'I Met Someone Who Claimed to Be the Devil… and I Think I Believe Them'. *R/Nosleep*. https://www.reddit.com/r/nosleep/comments/8chsch/i_met_someone_who_claimed_to_be_the_devil_and_i/.

Dennis Romero. 2013. *Elisa Lam Video*. YouTube Video. https://www.youtube.com/watch?v=3TjVBpyTeZM.

EaPAtbp. 2019. 'My Sugar Daddy Asks Me for Weird Favors'. *R/Nosleep*. https://www.reddit.com/r/nosleep/comments/diuucz/my_sugar_daddy_asks_me_for_weird_favors/.

Hunter, Jack. 2015. '"Between Realness and Unrealness": Anthropology, Paraphyschology and the Ontology of Non-Ordinary Realities'. *DISKUS* 17 (2): 4–20.

Ishak, Natasha. 2019. 'The Unsolved Mystery Behind The Disturbing Death Of Elisa Lam'. All That's Interesting. 5 April 2019. https://allthatsinteresting.com/elisa-lam-death.

Kinsella, Michael. 2011. *Legend-Tripping Online: Supernatural Folklore and the Search for Ong's Hat*. Jackson, Mississippi: University Press of Mississippi.

Lévi-Strauss, Claude. 1963. 'The Structural Study of Myth'. In *Structural Anthropology*, translated by C. Jacobson and B.G. Schoepf, 206–31. New York: Basic Books.

Lovecraft, H.P. 1973. *Supernatural Horror in Literature*. New York: Dover Publications.

Malinowski, Bronislaw. 1984. 'The Role of Myth in Life'. In *Sacred Narrative: Readings in the Theory of Myth*, edited by Alan Dundes, 193–206. Berkeley: University of California Press.

Northcote, Jeremy. 2004. 'Objectivity and the Supernormal: The Limitations of Bracketing Approaches in Providing Neutral Accounts of Supernormal Claims'. *Journal of Contemporary Religion* 19 (1): 85–98. https://doi.org/10.1080/1353790032000165131.

Otto, Rudolf. 1923. *The Idea of the Holy : An Inquiry into the Non-Rational Factor in the Idea of the Divine and Its Relation to the Rational*. London: Oxford University Press.

Park, Crystal L., Mary Alice Mills, and Donald Edmondson. 2012. 'PTSD as Meaning Violation: Testing a Cognitive Worldview Perspective.' *Psychological Trauma: Theory, Research, Practice, and Policy* 4 (1): 66–73. https://doi.org/10.1037/a0018792.

Index